OPTIONS TRADING

A Comprehensive Beginner's Guide to Learn the Basics and Realms of Options Trading

Table of Contents

Introduction

Options are unique in the world of financial trading. Buying and selling shares in a company is easy to understand, but trade is a little more complicated. It is a bit different to figure out how you can sell those shares before you buy them, and even make a profit from the reduction of that price. There are other things, rather than straightforward options. Derivatives are a good example. This means that you can buy things by ''deriving'' value for them from other things. If you take a future contract, as an example, you will see that the value of that contract changes as the price of its commodity underlies and varies. If that's the case, you can work with its derivatives. But when it comes to option trading, the definition is simple but complexity is multiplied. You can no longer look at the stock and see that shares are going up from 51 dollars to 57 dollars for example. And that won't necessarily mean that these 6 dollars of difference are your profit or your loss. With options, you pick from the same stock, but you choose an option, which has a distinct price (50, 55, 60 dollars, and so forth); and you also choose a specific time frame for the price to change. This date is your own estimation and the point is to pick wisely. With option trading, you often use your intuition. You can both buy or sell options and make income, but as you will see in the following chapters, this incomes often come with certain risks.

This Comprehensive Beginner's Guide to Learn the Basics and Realms of Options Trading is designed to point you in the right direction and to give you a full understanding of the many different definitions and strategies for options trading. You will find some basic ways in which you can set up your trading goals while keeping in mind all of the associated risks and rewards. Still, this guide should not be used as the only relevant source for options trading. Its purpose is to give you the basis from which you can improve your knowledge and skills in this area. The guide will provide you with an understanding of the possibilities that this kind of trade offers, and what strategies are the most effective ones.

There are different approaches that can explain many of the things that you will find in the book. However, this particular guide has collected the simplest yet most detailed observations. Many examples will hopefully help you understand and evaluate how options trading works in real life. Still, it would be wrong to assume that all of this will be enough to equip you with a complete knowledge for financial trading.

Being successful in trading requires hard work and a lot of studying, and this concept applies not only to option trading but to all financial actions of this kind. Be mindful about time scales in options trading, and remember that in the first few days or a few weeks you won't see any dramatic shifts in the value of your options. The reason for this is the fact that the trading profit actually comes from the loss of other traders. The way of getting profit is the same whether you trade derivatives, shares or options. The amount of money that goes around is smaller when you reduce the commissions that dealers and brokers take. These amounts of money are one of the reasons why many traders lose during the trade. You should educate yourself to avoid the fate of most of these brokers. Learn how to trade more smartly, as it will help you thrive or, at worst, to survive in the trading market. Consider these next pages simply as a start of your options trading journey in which you will be able to recognize and define the basic terms and strategies for your future career. It should give you the grounding that you need and motivate you to search forward and educate yourself further.

Chapter 1

Options - Definition, Buying and Selling Them; Advantages and Disadvantages of Trading Options

The option represents a contract in which the purchaser has the right to sell or buy an asset that is specified. This asset, however, has to be valued at a price that the purchaser will use to place the option on the market. A buyer can sell or keep the option on or before a certain date and even though he has the right to do so, the contract isn't obligatory. In this sense, the option is defined as a type of security, a bond or a binding contract to be more precise. However, this bond has its strictly defined properties and terms. Contracts for stock options can come in two forms: the first one is called the **call options** and the second one the **put options**. For both of these contracts, you gain the right but not the obligation to sell or buy that stock. Still, the price for the stock has to be predetermined. This predetermined price is also known as the strike price. Regardless of the type of these contracts (or options), there is an important feature known as an **expiration date**. This date is the ending time of an option because after that, the option becomes worthless. Investors can sell options before the expiration date and make a profit, but the value of the option will decrease the closer it comes to its expiration.

For example, in July 2014, the company we will name CBA is trading. The price of the options in trade is 10 dollars per share. If you decide to buy options from that stock by let's say 23rd of September, you could buy 100 shares for 12 dollars per share. Is there a reason for you to do this? One might think that the CBA Company is underpriced and that it will head upward. Anyhow, we will assume that you ended up buying those options and that now you wait a bit. There can be two outcomes. First, CBA Company starts trading shares again after 45 days and sells them for 15 dollars per share. This means that buying the stock for 12 dollars per share will mean a good profit in your case. On the other hand, there can be a second scenario. In this other scenario, CBA Company can start selling its shares again for a price below 12 dollars per share. This would mean that options that you bought can't be exercised and that they will eventually expire, and thus become worthless. So you either earn good money, or lose time and initial investment.

Terminology in options has another expression that is often used on the market. It refers to the price of the contract about options and it is known as the **premium**. This premium is considered to be in constant flux mostly because it is based on the activities of the security in its underlying operations and on the conditions of the market. The premium can be calculated using the following formula:

Premium= intrinsic value + time value.

In this case, intrinsic value equals the amount of the option being in the money, and the time value means that the price of the option will be higher if there is more time before its expiration. Keep in mind that evaluating your own option for selling means that you need to deduct the premium from your profit. Only after you do that can you create a proper value for the option you want to trade further.

Selling, buying, and writing options

In the world of options trading, you have two possible roles: to be the buyer or the seller. Buying underlying instruments such as underlying stock is the right you get if you purchase a call option. However, for that right to be legit, you need to purchase this stock for a strike price that is specified before the options' expiration date. Contrarily, if you buy a put option, the situation is different. In this case, you get the right to sell the stock rather than buy it. This stock also needs to be sold before the options expire and at the strike price. Both ways you have the choice of selling the option to someone else or you can just let it reach its expiration date and become worthless.

Still, if by any chance you write options and want to sell them, you have some terms to fulfill first. There are obligatory requirements for an option contract in the case where the buyer wants to exercise them at any point. This means that if you sell a call option that you wrote, you also have to provide the underlying asset that goes with that call option. Both of these things have to be sold together at the strike price to the buyer. In case you want to buy a specific option and its asset - you have to buy that whole stock also at the strike price. If you want to write options, you need to keep in mind that exercising the contract is entirely the buyer's choice. So if the buyer decides to exercise that choice, you need to be prepared to fulfill the terms that were given with the contract. Still, there are some workarounds in case you really don't want to have any obligations to the buyer. You can buy another contract. But be careful, because this contact must be appropriate to offset the obligation you had to the person who bought your previous option.

Advantages and disadvantages of trading options

Once you understand the basic meaning of options, you will see that there are both advantages and disadvantages. One of the main advantages in options trading is the possibility to increase your money and use leverage or to use hedging as a mechanism to deal with the threats that you might face. On the contrary, there are also a few risks that shouldn't be overlooked. These risks are often referred to as disadvantages of the options trading. They should be carefully weighed every time before you start trading.

Advantages

Leverage is considered to be one of the main advantages of options. It represents the ability to make a considerable amount of profit without big upfront capital. The use of financial leverage in options trading is one of the most significant factors in gaining a bigger profit while minimizing capital that needs to be invested. Investors use leverage all the time, especially in the initial stages of the trade. Let's take an example of you wanting to invest 1.000

dollars. You use that money and you buy options in CCC company, let's say. At the moment you were buying the stock, the company was selling options for 10 dollars per share, which means that you were able to get 100 shares. Let's not take broker commissions and fees into consideration here because it is simpler to calculate. If the value of the options in that company increases up to 12.50 dollars per share, you can sell your stock and gain 250 dollars of pure profit. Without deducting the brokerage fees, we can say that you earned 25 percent more money on your initial expense.

Contrarily, if you know how to use leverage properly, your returns and your profit can be much higher. So, if the strike price for your stock in was 10 dollars for each 10 dollar share, this would mean that you could buy 1.000 stock shares or 100 options. If we add the rise of the stock value to 12.50 dollars per share you could use terms of your option contract and buy shares for the price of 10 dollars but sell them for 12.50 dollars. When you sum everything up, you would earn 1.500 dollars or 150% more than your initial investment. This case represents a classic example of the power that leverage has in trading. When using options, the person who trades can invest without borrowing money from other people. Options and leverage also allow that person to use small amounts of initial capital to control more shares.

Hedging - otherwise known as the limitation of the risk - is one more advantage of options. Hedging gives a kind of safeguard to the investors and their position and insures their money during the fluctuation in prices. This is an especially important feature if the investor wants to trade without altering the underlying position and he uses options as a protective shield against the price drops. It is a way of keeping its portfolio safe. Another name for it on the trading market is hedging which is usually used as a great strategy in risk management.

For example, if you have 100 shares from before in CCC Company, you might be worried that they will head for a fall on the market. One of the solutions is that you get a put option for that stock. This put option will enable you to sell another option for its strike price at that moment even though the price of the stock reduces on the regular market. This means that you have insured yourself for the premium price and you won't experience any losses if the value of the options starts to get lower. Hedging is considered to be a conservative strategy that is used by investors to limit their potential loss of profit while trading.

Disadvantages

One of the biggest disadvantages of options trading is its **levels of risk**. These levels depend on your role of being a writer or a holder of the options. This way we can say that there are two levels of risk. When you are a holder of the option, your biggest risk is that you can lose your premiums whether it is the entire amount of it or just a part. Also, if you let the option expire and it becomes worthless, you can lose your whole principal amount. On the other hand, writing an option carries even bigger risks. As a writer, you are exposed to multiple kinds of losses. For example, if you wrote an option for uncovered calls, there is an unlimited risk where you can lose the underlying security for your profit.

Another disadvantage is something that we call the **intrinsic value.** This value is not the same for a stock or the options that you'd potentially buy. For example, if the option is ''at the money'' or ''out of the money'' at the moment, it means that it doesn't have intrinsic value that is real. The only value that this kind of option has is its time value. Still, time as value tends to decline the closer the option gets to its date of expiration. Keep in mind that we will explain the terms ''at the money'' and ''out of the money'' in some of the following chapters.

Options have their own unique risks that no other item has on the trading market. This risk is qualified as time decay. It means that the option loses its value the closer it gets to its expiration date. The contract becomes worthless if it isn't exercised using the ''in the money'' strategy. If during the time frame of the option there were some unexpected turns with the security, which we label as an underlying one, the investor is threatened with the risk of losing all of the capital he invested in the trade. With stocks it is different. You can just wait it out, but with options, you can't. This is one of the main reasons why options are sometimes called wasting assets also.

Tax implications are also one of the elements that you need to consider before entering any trade or investing in buying any options. Options represent short-term investments, which mean that they are taxed differently from long term ones. Still, gains of your investment can be offset if you experience loss in your trading. If that is the case, taxes can be observed as an advantage. Anyhow, it is not recommended to make any move without consulting with a tax advisor first. The best way of managing this kind of risk is to have a predetermined tax-saving strategy.

In the end, trading options is used to make big profits by positioning yourself on the market intelligently and most often with leverage. Contrarily, every trade comes with its own risks of different levels and it requires that the investor has to be present and knowledgeable about the market situation all the time. Even though options are short-term investments, it doesn't mean that you can buy them and forget about them. Investors who get and forget the investment are not suitable for this kind of trade because with options you have to be present all the time, especially since they have unique time constraints.

Chapter 2

Variety of Options and Their Styles

Available options come in many different types and styles. In this chapter, we will overview some basic expressions that everyone interested in options trading should know, and talk in more detail about all of the existing option types.

Firstly, there are **Call Options**. These options provide you with the right to buy stock labeled as an underlying one. With Call Options, you can buy not only stocks but also commodities, bonds or any other instrument that has a specified price, otherwise known as the strike price, within a certain timeframe. As was previously mentioned, the Call Options contract gives you the right to buy, but you don't have an obligation to do so. A person who is bullish on the stock is usually the investor who expects the value of the stock to increase shortly. This kind of investor buys call options and manages them in the specified time frame. Again, let's take an example.

Let's say that the investor we will name Mr. B thinks that next month CCC Company will have bigger earnings for the stock, and the stock will have a higher value. In this case, Mr. B buys a call option for the CCC Company's stock for 20 dollars for example.

The contract of the option has a term that Mr. B can buy up to 100 shares from CCC Company within the next two months. The strike price for these shares within this time frame is 100 dollars. So, if the value of the stock goes below 100 dollars in the next period, Mr. B won't exercise his option, which means that, he will lose his original 20 dollars of investment (remember, if the option is not exercised within the specific time frame, or two months in this particular case, the contract expires and becomes worthless). On the other hand, if the value of the stock goes over 100 dollars, and the next price is 130 dollars, for example, Mr. B can exercise his option. He can now buy the stock for 100 dollars and sell it for 130 dollars on the market. The risk that Mr. B took paid off and he earned a significant profit.

Secondly, we have **Put Options.** These options have opposite traits from the Call Options. Put Options represent the contract in which the purchaser has the right to sell his or her stocks. These stocks, like all of the others, have to be sold for the strike price (a price that's been specified for a certain time). Put Options, like Call Options, give the right to sell, but they are not obligatory. Now we can return to Mr. B and observe him as an investor who is bearish on a certain stock.

In this example, Mr. B thinks that the price of the stock he is interested in will decrease and, in that case, he will purchase a put option. According to Mr. B, the stock that CCC Company has is overpriced and its value will go lower in the next two months. Let's say that Mr. B buys a Put Option on this stock for 20 dollars again.

Contract of the Put Option gives Mr. B a chance to sell the stock he bought from CCC Company for 120 dollars in the next 60 days. So if the stock value increases more than 120 dollars per share, Mr. B won't have to exercise his Put Option, the time frame will pass and the option will become worthless which means that he would lose only his initial capital of 20 dollars. However, if the value of the stock goes down, and the price goes from 120 dollars to 90 dollars, for example, the Put Option will be exercised and Mr. B can sell this stock for 120 dollars per share. Once again, he judged correctly and he has made a considerable profit.

How to make a profit using Call Options and Put Options

There are many ways for a trader to use Call Options and Put Options and be successful in the process. The best way to show some of the most efficient ways to use these options is by using real numbers. Imagine you want to buy shares from US Bank. Let's suppose that the bank currently sells them for the price of 200 dollars per share and that you conclude that this number is going to go up since the shares are underpriced. Let's also suppose that the predicted amount of time that the shares will need to increase their value is a few months from now. At the moment, you don't have enough capital to buy 100 shares from the US Bank. However, you still want to make some profit from the stock that will rise in value according to your estimation. If this is the case, you can use Call Option and buy it for the stock. This way you reduce the cost and you pay only a fraction of the real stock price. Once that you purchased the Call Option, you gained the right to buy 100 shares of US Bank stock for 200 dollars per share in the next two months.

One of your doubts might immediately be how are you supposed to buy that stock for 200 dollars per share in the next 60 days when you don't have the initial amount of money for that in the first place? Well, the thing is that you are not under obligation to actually buy the stock if you want to make money. If your estimation is correct and in the next period the value of the stock goes over 200 dollars per share, the Call Option that you bought would increase in value too. In other words, your option contract value rises with the value of the stock price. Keeping this in mind, you get the opportunity to sell your Call Options contract to make money, not the shares. That is the real connection because once when the stock price rises, your contract is worth a lot more than the money you invested to buy it.

A similar thing happens if you purchase the Put Options contract. The only difference is that your estimation has to be decreased in the stock value rather than prices going higher. Once when the underlying security price goes down, the price of your Put Option will go up. The more that the stock price falls the more expensive your contract becomes. Using options in both cases means that you can make a profit regardless of the rise or fall of the stock prices.

Option Styles

In the previous section, we defined the two main option types. In this section, we will discuss different styles of options. There are various styles of options used in the trader's market and it is very important to understand them. However, most of the options that are used in everyday trading belong to one of the main styles -

American style or European style. These two categories are often called vanilla options and their main difference is the time of execration for both types of options.

The first style of options that we will introduce is also one of the two that are used most often. These options are called **American Options** and their main characteristic is that they can be exercised at any point as long as the option hasn't reached its expiration date. American Options are also considered to be the most frequent type of contract traded on the market when it comes to future exchanges.

European Options, on the other hand, have a different excretion policy. The expiration date of the option has to be defined in the contract, which means that the option can be exercised only during that specific period. Type of market called ''over the counter' or OTC for short is the market in which European Options are traded the most.

However, the value of American and European Options is calculated differently. Additionally, the expiration date is also different for each of these styles. For American Options, the expiration date is pre-determined before the investor purchases the contract. The American Option always expires on the third Saturday of the following month. Contrarily, the European Option becomes worthless on Friday – a day before the third Saturday of the specified month. There are a few similarities between these so-called vanilla options too. They both have the rule of buying and selling at the strike price and they both include pay-off. Furthermore, whether you calculate pay off for the Call or Put

Options, the process is the same and it usually means that the strike price for these options is the same most of the time.

As we already mentioned, vanilla options are the two main styles that investor use while trading. However, many other option styles should be aware of. These other styles that are not that frequent are called **Exotic Options**.

Bermuda Options, for example, are a style of option that qualifies as something in between American and European versions. The key difference is that Bermuda Options can be exercised on more than a few dates as long as the contract is valid.

On the other hand, there are **Barrier Options**. These options are the most different ones so far and the reason is that there is a border that needs to be passed to get the payoff for the underlying security price. This is the case for both Call and Put Options. Barrier Options are divided into four categories:

  · **"Down and Out" Barrier Options** – the purchaser of this option has the right (but like in every other case no obligation) to buy or sell shares, depending on the type of option that he chooses. The condition is that whether these underlying assets are bought or sold, it has to be done using already determined strike price. The strike price, however, mustn't go lower than a barrier that is pre-determined with the option contract until the expiration date. If by any chance the price of the owner's shares go below this barrier

17

the option loses every value, and that is why it was named ''down and out''

- **"Down and In" Barrier Options** – this option is the total opposite of the ''down and out'' category. An investor who has this option has to know that the only time that ''down and in barrier'' has a value is when the price of all assets that are underlying and allowed to be purchased by the contract goes below the barrier that was pre-determined for that particular option until it expires. The purchaser has the right to sell or buy shares (again, depending on the type of purchased option) if the barrier was crossed. Like in the previous category, this trade also has to be done before the expiration date is due and at the strike price.

- **''Up and Out'' Barrier Options** – this category of Barrier Options is similar to ''down and out''. The main distinction is the fact that the barrier itself is placed differently. In this case, ''up and out'' means that if the price of any underlying asset that is bought increases above the barrier that is predetermined by the contract, the option will lose its value.

- **''Up and In'' Barrier Options** – Unlike ''up and out'', this category has similarities with ''down and in'' options rather than ''down and out''. The barrier, in this case, is set above the current value of any underlying asset purchased by the investor. The only time that this kind of option carries value is when the price of the stock reaches the placed barrier before the contract expires.

Basket Options are the third kind of Exotic Options we will review in this section. There is another name for these options – that is **rainbow options**. They represent a contract in which the price is formed relying on the value of at least two underlying assets. If the option holder wants to exercise the Basket Option, it has to take the value of all assets into consideration.

Capped Style Options are a type of Exotic Options in which we have to pre-determine the amount of profit that can be gathered by exercising it. This option has a provision that says that if a certain value is reached (this certain value has to be determined upon the option purchase), the option will be exercised automatically. The main characteristic of this option is the opportunity for the option writer to determine the maximum amount of capital that can be lost in case something goes wrong.

Compound Option is a type of Exotic Option that actually enables you to buy an option with another option. They are sometimes called the ''split fee'' options because the one who purchases them has to pay two kinds of premiums, one that is paid before and one after the option is exercised.

Look-Back Option is an Exotic Option that provides its buyer the right to sell or buy its underlying assets for the lowest or the highest price whether he has Put Option or Call Option to exercise.

Asian Options are contracts in which the payoff of the underlying security is subjected to the average price for the predetermined amount of time. These options are otherwise known as ''the average options''.

Another style of Options that has unusual terms is **Binary Options**. With these options the payout can have only two outcomes: you can get a fixed amount of money or you won't get anything. Binary Options have two categories. The first one is called ''cash or nothing'', and the other one is called ''asset or nothing''. ''Cash or nothing'' means that if the option expires ''in the money'' the owner will get the fixed amount of profit. Alternatively, the option purchaser will get the value of a security that is underlying in case that his option is in the ''asset or nothing'' category. These categories are often referred to as Digital Options or, as we previously mentioned, ''all or nothing'' or ''fixed return'' options. The main advantage of these contracts is that the holder is sure about the amount that he can potentially receive even before he bought the option. Still, the biggest disadvantage of Binary Options is that once that you buy them, you can't sell them until they expire.

Forward Start Options are a style of options in which the holder starts its trade with the strike price that is undetermined. The key characteristic of this option is that it enables you to define the strike price of your assets in the future.

Long-term Equity Anticipation Securities or LEAPS for short are a style of options that is basically the same as regular ones. The only difference is that LEAPS options have longer dates for expiration and they can go up to three years. If you want to invest your money long-term LEAPS has the advantage of giving you much more time for an underlying stock than the other options. This way you can manage your capital in directions that you estimate to be correct.

Index Options are options that enable you to buy on a stock index too. This way you are not limited to buy only individual security options, with Index Options you have access to the whole groups of stocks on the market. These options can be used in many strategies, whether they are speculative for investors or conservative. They are flexible and they can be adjusted to any market (bear or bull). The most frequent index options purchased from traders are European Options.

Chapter 3

Valuation and Option Pricing

Determining the value of the premiums and the price that has to be paid for an option depends on a few factors. One of the main ones is the underlying security's current price. We can split options into three categories based on their underlying assets' current value. These categories are known as: ''in the money'', ''at the money'', or ''out of the money.

In The Money (ITM) - This term means that you have an option which worth is based on the value of its underlying asset at the moment. If that is the case for Call Option, for example, it means that the strike price of that option is lower than the stock price on the market. Let's say that the strike price of your Call Option is 30 dollars, and the price for the stock on the market is 35 dollars at the moment. In this situation, your Call Option is referred to as ''in the money''. Contrarily, if you have a Put Option that you classify as ''in the money'' it would mean that the price of your option is 35 dollars while the stock price on the market is 30 dollars. In both cases, the same principle applies - the bigger difference between the current and the strike price means that the option value is larger.

**At The Money** *(ATM)* - Whether you hold a Put Option or a Call Option, the prices for stock and the strike are the same. If that is the case, the option is referred to as ''at the money''. For example, let's suppose that the strike price of the Call Option is 50 dollars. Also, the underlying share for that option is traded on the market for the same amount of 50 dollars per share. If these values are equal, it is said that the option doesn't have any intrinsic value which is an in time value. Intrinsic value means that the contract will have more value as long as it is far away from its expiration and its value will decrease as it approaches the expiration date.

Out of the Money **(OTM)** – As the name suggests, the phrase ''out of the money'' means that the contract has expired and that your option has no value. This conclusion is also based on the price of the underlying assets in the current market. The purchaser usually doesn't exercise this kind of option. We say that the Call Option (for example) is ''out of the money'' if the underlying stock on the current market has a lower price than the strike price of the Call Option. So if the strike value of the option is 35 dollars and stock shares are traded for 30 dollars per share, we will label that option as ''out of the money''. This happens because the holder is unable to exercise his right to buy the shares at the strike price, thus they are cheaper to obtain on the regular market. On the contrary, the Put Options are considered to be out of the money if the current market value is above the strike price of underlying assets.

So if the strike price for options is 30 dollars per option and value of the stock is 35 dollars per share at the moment, we say that the

Put Option is "out of the money" here. Selling the stock for a lower price than the market value isn't beneficial to the investor, which is why he wouldn't exercise his Put Option in this case. Just like ATM, OTM doesn't have intrinsic value, which means that the price of its option decreases with the approach of the expiration date.

Difference between Intrinsic Value and Time Value

Options premiums have two main components. These components are intrinsic value and time value. Intrinsic value represents the difference in price between the stock market and the strike price for that same stock. The intrinsic value will be positive if you have "in the money" option and it will be zero if you have "at the money" or "out of the money" options. If you have the first kind of options, intrinsic value will rise along with the difference between the two mentioned prices. Calculating the intrinsic value is easy. For example, we take a stock that is priced for 50 dollars. You bought a Call Option and paid the strike price of 45 dollars for it. The intrinsic value of your Call Option in this example is 5 dollars. But if the price of the stock was 45 dollars or even less than that, that would mean that your Call Option lost its value, therefore it doesn't have any intrinsic value.

The second important component that we mentioned above is the time value of an option. This value is directly connected to the options expiration date. As we already explained several times, when the expiration date of an option passes without that option being exercised or sold, that option becomes worthless. This is one of the main arguments for labeling option trading as highly-risked ventures. To be able to understand it better, you should think of options expiration dates as time decays. To put it simply, the shorter the option has before it becomes worthless, the less value in the time it has. This means that the value of your option will decrease with time and even more if the underlying assets have lower prices or just don't change their value at all.

We can say that time decay represents one of the most critical elements for the trade and it has to be carefully observed by those who invest in options trading. Unlike the intrinsic value that was easy to calculate, time value requires a little work. Since there is already an established the date of expiration, the option already has a determined amount of time to move in the direction that the holder wants to. Generally speaking, the less you wait for the expiration date to come, the smaller the value of your option. The same principle applies to the premium too - the more time you have before the option expires, the bigger your premium will be. If you think about it, it is logical, because more time means more chance to achieve some goals.

Models for Option Pricing
Options have several models that are used to establish their value at the current market. We will overview some of the most important and the most frequently used ones.

The Black-Sholes Model is considered to be the one that investors use the most to determine the price of their options. This model was first used in 1973 and further developed by three economists named

Myron Sholes, Fischer Black, and Robert Merton. The Black-Sholes model calculates the value of the European option and the formula used for its calculation is quite complicated. That is why most of the investors don't want to do them alone so they usually use online calculators that are specified for options trading and that is always available.

Another model that is actually a variation of the first formula is known as the **Cox-Rubenstein Binomial options model**. It doesn't use only the expiration date to determine the price of the underlying security, but the period. This is why this model is tightly connected to the pricing of American options. As you have already seen, American options can be exercised at any point in time as long as it is within the time frame of the contract. Just like with the Black-Sholes model, it is rather difficult to calculate Cox-Rubinstein Binomial option value by hand. Luckily, the internet has many different calculators that can simplify the process.

Put/call parity is the model that is referring to the relationship that the strike prices and date of expirations have with the Call Options and Put Options. However, this model for calculating the value of the options is used only for European style. The definition says that ''the value of a call option at one strike price, implies a fair value for the corresponding put and vice versa.''

In other words, this model uses the principle of the same amount of return, which means that the stock positions and the options must have the same return to achieve balance. If that is not the case it could lead to arbitrage or the possibility to provide profit from a difference in prices, which would allow investors to gain risk-free money. This model is often used as a test for the investors to check if they priced their options fairly. In case you want to double-check this, there are many tools on various trading platforms that can analyze parity for both Put Options and Call Options.

What are the Greeks and why is it important to know them?
If you want to enter the world of options trading you need to be aware of terms that are commonly known as the Greeks. The Greeks represent values that traders use to determine different positions of options and to evaluate the level of risk that is involved with their trade of interest.

Delta is a value used to measure the sensitivity of the option's price and it is related to the underlying assets that traders want to acquire. Delta is portrayed as several points that the option will move on the market and every point means that there has been a change in the stock's underlying security. This value is the most frequently used Greek, thus the one you need to know the most. Delta informs the holder how the value of his or her option will change using the fluctuation of the stock prices. The usual value used to express Delta is somewhere between 0.0 and 1.0 if you have Call Options. If you, however, have Put Options, the value of Delta will be given as a number between 0.0 and -1.0 Keep in mind that Deltas are commonly whole numbers rather than just decimals and the closer that Delta value is to 1 or -1, it means that your option is more valuable.

Gamma is a value that determines the change of Delta for the particular option. This change happens when the underlying assets start to change their prices. Gamma is mostly used when the investor wants to see how the options' price fluctuates and how deep its investment is in or out of the money. When the Gama increases in its value it means that the option starts to get closer to being ''at the money''. Contrarily, if the option path goes in the direction of being ''out of the money'' or ''into the money'' Gama will start to decrease.

Rho is a Greek used for estimation of the change that happens with the options price when the interest rate and premium changes. Generally speaking, if the interest rate increases on Call Options, the premium is supposed to rise. On the contrary, if the interest rate increases on Put Option, their premium will go lower.

Vega is a value that measures how much the option is sensitive to the volatility of the stock's underlying assets. In other words, the option will be more impacted by the rise of the volatility price if there is more time before it expires. Still, increased volatility means that the option price will increase too.

Theta is used to determine the reaction of the option on the time decay. Theta measures the value that the option loses every day while being closer to its expiration. A large number of platforms that are used by options traders offer Greek values that are up to date and for every type, style or category of the contract you might be interested in.

Chapter 4

Before Using Your Algos

Now that we have reviewed some of the basic definitions, types, styles, and categories of options, we should focus on some of the first things that you will face when you begin with your trades.

Exchanging Options

Becoming a trader generally means that you are about to become a part of a very wide community. However, option trades can be made on many exchanges and you need to know which ones are regulated. We already explained that options are contracts, and through the previous chapters we determined that those contracts are mostly standardized which means that it is possible to trade them between different exchanges. This implies that most of the options can be found on multiple exchanging platforms. In the further text, we will mention eleven exchanges that can be found for the option's trading. They are MIAX Options Exchange, NYSE Amex Options, C2 Options Exchange, NASDAQ OMX BX, BOX Options Exchange, International Securities Exchange (ISE), NYSE Arca Options, NASDAQ OMX PHLX, BATS Options Exchange, NASDAQ Options Market, and the Chicago Board Options Exchange (CBOE).

OCC or the Options Clearing Corporation is a company founded in 1973. OCC represents something like a clearinghouse for all options contracts ever issued. Also, this company is the one that is in charge of releasing and guaranteeing for every option contract made now or in the future. This is why investors feel secure in trading options. Options Clearing Corporation acts as a kind of legal insurance that everyone involved in the trade will get its premiums and that everything will be done according to the terms and regulations described in the contract that a trader gets with the option purchase. Still, if something goes wrong, the jurisdiction passes on to the Securities and Exchange Commission otherwise known as SEC.

Trading Account

The very first thing you need to start trading options is your own brokerage account. There is a big choice of firms that offer services of account opening and more often they include packages with broker discount and full service in their offers. Depending on the level of knowledge you have and how much advice you are going to need you can choose some of the options. Usually, the companies that provide lower fees don't give personal advice. On the other hand, the most successful firms on the market can provide you with not only personalized advice, but with all the necessary tools that will help you make better decisions with your investments. Here is a list of some of the most successful brokerage companies that were, or still are, on the market:

OptionsHouse – www.optionshouse.com

Merrill Edge – www.merrilledge.com

TradeStation – www.tradestation.com

Fidelity Investments - www.fidelity.com

TD Ameritrade - www.tdameritrade.com

OptionsXpress – www.optionsxpress.com

Place Trade – www.placetrade.com

E*Trade – www.etrade.com

tradeMonster – www.trademonster.com

Interactive Brokers – www.interactivebrokers.com

Charles Schwab - www.schwab.com

Keep in mind that once you select your brokerage company, you will have to select a type of account for your further actions. Mostly there are two types of accounts so you can choose to open either a margin account or a cash account.

If you choose to open a margin account, you can use collaterals and finance your transactions by borrowing money for your investments. If you, however, choose to open a cash account, you will have the opportunity to trade your options and make investments only with the money that is available on your account. In case you decide to go with a margin account, you will have to leave a deposit. The minimum amount of money that has to be left as a deposit for each brokerage company is 2000 dollars; otherwise, you can't even open the account. On the contrary, for a cash account, you either has to put a symbolic deposit or none at all. Additionally, every brokerage house has different rules about the number of assets and money that you need to maintain your account.

If you ever receive something that is called a margin call, it means that the amount that you have on your account went below the required limit. A margin call is a kind of reminder that you need to add either assets or money to be able to work with your account. If these conditions aren't met, the company has the right to liquidate all your assets. This is why you must always keep track of the margin requirements of your brokerage house.

When you finish setting up your account, there is another step that you need to take before trading. There is an option agreement that needs to be completed before any trader starts its work with options. The purpose of this agreement is to provide and to outline all possible actions with the purchased options. It also has to give you a basic understanding of the risk levels that you might meet during the trading process and familiarize yourself with your investment ability to deal with losses. When the agreement is completed, the company does the next step and assigns you in for optional approval. There are few levels of optional approval and since there isn't any standard for them, we shortlisted the most typical ones. The first level usually offers longer Put Options that are protective and it covers Call Options too. The second level fully covers both Call and Put Options. The third typical level usually covers straddles and spreads, while the fourth level mostly refers to uncovered Call and Put Options that are also known as ''the naked'' options.

If the investor doesn't have much experience, the brokerage firm usually assignees him or her to the first or the second level. This way they protect the inexperienced trader from losing all of his or her money. New traders mostly have limited knowledge about the risk levels of the trade and their understanding of the market is usually not good enough. Brokerage houses not only protect their new investors but they also protect their own company from suffering ant loses. The most frequent brokerage action is to help their clients leveling up their trending abilities and improve the status and income for both – the trader and the company.

Placing the orders and determining their types

Another important thing that you mustn't forget when entering the world of trade is the ability to place your order. Beginners often come to the wrong conclusion that it is enough to just pick which kind of options you want and that's it- you just sell them and buy them when you think is suitable. Unfortunately, options trading is not that simple. You need to decide and follow one of the four option types of orders. These types are: buy to close but to open, sell to close and sell to open. When you choose which type of order you will use for your trade you have to decide will you fulfill it through the market order or you will go through a limit order instead. Another important thing is that you shouldn't forget to notify your broker what will be the timing of your order.

Now we will overview all breakdown order types:

The first one is named ''buy to open''. This order is the one that is placed most often, and it is the simplest order for options. It enables you to buy a contract and to determine a new position of the option.

The second option order is called ''buy to close''. This offer is used to close the existing contract and to end the short position of the option. This kind of order is placed if you had a distinctive short sold contract and you wanted to leave that position, thus get out and end the contract. For example, if there is a subsequent decrease in the value of the options that you have sold, you can buy them back for that lower price if you place a ''buy to close'' order and therefore lock in the amount of profit that you can make. Differently, if you sold your options and their value went up in the meantime, you can ease up your loses if you use ''buy to close'' order and buy your options back. This way you prevent further loss of your money. Keep in mind that taking a short position means that you can make a profit only when the value of the options that you sold goes down. Once their value starts going up, you will lose your position.

The third type of order that you can see is ''sell to open'' type of order. It is used for opening the position on contracts that the investor wants to short sell. For instance, you can use ''sell to open'' order if you want to sell a Covered Call Option.

Last but not the least, there is a ''sell to close'' order. This order enables you to exit any position by reselling your option and its contract with it. Actually, this order is mostly used only for selling the contracts that you have already owned. ''Sell to close'' order can be used for both Call Options and Put Options too.

Fill Orders and its types

Once that you decided which type of order you want to use, the next thing is to see what options you have for filling out that order. There are several ways to do so. You can either choose to do it with limit orders, market orders, stop limit orders and stop orders.

Limit order is a type of fulfillment which allows you to execute your trade at a price that is not higher (if you trade with Call Options) or lower (if you trade with Put Options) than your already designed price. This way you protect yourself from obtaining options that have a higher value than you anticipated or lower price in case you want to buy options instead of selling them.

Market order type of fulfillment enables you to fill the order you have placed by using the price that is currently on the market. This type of filling orders carries some risks since the price can often move quickly. This means that you might end up having to buy contracts at a higher price than you thought or, on the contrary sell your option contracts for a price that is lower than you anticipated.

Stop-Limit gives you the chance to fill out the order by combining the different features of limit orders and stop orders. This further leads to the definition of the stop order that says that this order is filled once that the price of an option gets to its stop price.

Timing of your orders

Placing the order has some additional requirements and one of them is to tell for how long your order will be valid. This is also called the timing or the duration of your order. There are six types of the order timing and we will briefly overview them. They are all or none, day order, good until canceled, fill or kill, good until date, and immediate or cancel.

If you choose all or none order, it means that you have to fill all of your orders completely, otherwise none of the orders won't be filled. For example, if you want to get 30 contracts for a specific price the broker you work with can obtain only 25 for that value it means that your order will not be processed at all. Keep in mind that this timing can't expire until the end of the day, which is not the case with the day order. Still, if you want you can cancel this timing for fulfillment anytime you want.

Contrarily, the day order timing represents a kind of order in which you must fill out everything that is requested by the end of the trading day. If you start the order during that one trading day and you don't finish, your order will be automatically canceled.

On the other hand, you can use *fill or kill order* if your choice is to set a kind of all or none request. This order, however, comes with some additional requirements that have no worth if you don't fill the order immediately.

If your order is GTC or *good till canceled* it means that the only way to cancel your order is for you to cancel it personally. If you don't do it, it will stay active until it is filled.

If you, however, decide to go with the *good till date* kind of *order*, GTD for short, your order will be valid until the time you specified in the placement expires. If the order is not filled by that time it gets canceled automatically.

And the sixth way to decide on the time limit to your order is to go with the *immediate or cancel kind of order*. Immediate or cancel is actually very similar to fill or kill kind of order, but there is one key difference. The main distinction between the two is the fact that only those parts of the order, which are filled immediately, won't be canceled. All other contracts or some other elements of the order lose their value if not filled by that time.

Options chains and making trades

Options chains are one of the most important sources of information for any trader who wants to work with options. You can usually find many relevant and real-time information about option chains either consulting your broker or finding the information on several financial websites. Still, you should know how to read an option chain if you see it. Here is a short overview:

The options chain is usually portrayed as a chart. The top of the chart in most of the cases is a place in which you will see the exchange name for the option, its underlying stock name, ticker symbol that it has, the volume of the option and of course its current price on the market. Columns of the option chain chart mostly are divided so you can find details about options strike price, its symbol, its change, the volume of the option, and additionally its ask, bid and open interest.

The strike price of the option is usually placed in the first column while the second column is the place where you'll find the options symbol. In these options chain, charts information is displayed for both Call Options and Put Options and their strike prices. The next column of the chart has the purpose of providing the current price of the option on the market, or how much money is a buyer willing to pay for the option. Contrarily, the ask column gives you the info about the price for which the option holder is willing to sell you the option. When it comes to the next column or volume in this case, it represents the number of contracts that were traded on the website or brokerage report for that day. Last but not least, the open interest column shows how many opened contracts are left for that trading day.

When you enter the real process of order execution you will realize that the process itself doesn't have some hidden or complex procedures. It is actually very clear and straightforward and the process is the same for online trades and the trades made over the phone.

So, as we already discussed, first of all, you need to place your trade. To do so you will need to decide what type of option you will work with (you have to choose either Put Option or Call Option). Then you need to determine your option symbol. After that, it is important to notify which fill order type you will work with. Is it going to buy to close, but to open, sell to close or sell to open type? Other information you need to provide if you want to place your order is to determine the strike price for your option and of course its expiration date. In the end, you need to establish what amount of money you are willing to pay if buying the option, which is actually choosing between a limit order and market order. Be mindful of the timing of the order too. You will have to choose between day orders, fill or kill order, and so forth.

The next step is to confirm your order, but before you do that, don't forget to double-check all the information that you posted while placing your trade. All data have to be correct because later there might not be a possibility to change it. When you submit the order that you placed, most frequently you will have to wait for the confirmation. When the order is placed on the market you will get the notification that it is pending to be executed and that it must be filled to be executed in the first place.

This leads us to the next thing, which is the execution of your trade. The trade depends on the details you provided while placing the order. It means that it could take a few minutes or even a few days until you receive the information that the trade has been executed. Once the order is considered to be filled the website or the brokerage house notifies you and it shows you the price of that execution.

When you do all that, the next phase is to keep track of your positions and follow through the plan that you made before you entered trading at all.

Tools for trading

There are many different tools that you can find to help you with your trading. Brokers often offer not only tools but calculators too so the whole process is much easier and it doesn't matter if you are new in options trading or not.

Before you enter any trade, the most useful tool that you can use is research and find the data analysis about the underlying stocks that you are interested in. This data can be a price history of the stock for example; they can also be something like earning reports, volatility, and so forth.

The next valuable tool for you can be paper trading. This is a simulated environment for trading in which you can practice and get some experience bore you really start investing your money and do the trades with real risks.

Calculator for options is a tool that calculates the profit that you might potentially earn or the losses that you might experience during the trade. This calculator also gives you the Greek values that are necessary for your trades.

Screener for the options enables you to narrow down the options you have because you can screen and place them using different criteria such as the forecast of the market, volatility or something else.

An options chain is a tool that can show you all a series of options that are offered for a stock whether you are looking for Call Options or Put Options. They also show the premiums that you might get, the volume of the offered options and another characteristic already mentioned above.

Overview of Trading Strategies

One of the most important tasks that you must do before you start trading options is to decide what kind of strategy you will use. The best way to establish the best one that suits your needs is to set some goals for your investment and make sure that the strategy will help you reach them. If you already own some stocks and you want to protect your investment from loss of value or ultimately protect yourself for losing capital, you will naturally choose a different strategy from a person that wants to gain larger profit by using leverage to increase it and maximizing the benefits that options provide.

When you are a beginner, the best way to approach the options trading is to start with some simple techniques that will help you to achieve positive results and upgrade your knowledge and experience during the process. As you become a more experienced trader and when you start feeling more confident in your trading skills, you can try some of the more complex strategies.

One of the most popular simple strategies for investors of all levels and financial capacity is buying Call Options. This strategy allows the purchaser to buy options for the stock that he thinks will have a higher price shortly. In case the price of the stock does go higher the premium and the strike price paid before the options' date of expiration is going to be profitable for the option holder.

However, if investor's estimation goes wrong and the prices go lower than anticipated, he or she can lose all of the premiums and even their initial investment. Most of the Call Options and their contracts are sold before they expire especially when the premiums are increasing. Still, if one of your goals is to buy the underlying security, you can do it at any point as long as the option hasn't expired. Since everyone has the same objective of making a profit, you should keep in mind that for this strategy to work you need to have good timing and the ability to recognize the point in which you should terminate the contract because if you wait longer than you should you risk your investment.

The same happens if the stock price doesn't go up as fast or as high as you estimated. It can happen that you can't exercise your option at all or that the option becomes worthless in the meantime. Some investors don't buy stock on margins but Call Options instead by offering the same leverage utility. However, this kind of trade is less risky for them. They act like that because when you buy a stock on margin even if the stock falls, the consequence is that you will receive a margin call. This means that you will have to add money on your account or the brokerage company will liquidate all your assets to get everything right. This way the purchaser of the Call Options has only the risk of losing premium rather than losing the whole investment.

Put buying is a simple strategy that is very similar to the call buying one. The main difference is that in this strategy you estimate that the price of the stock will decrease. As an investor, you can use this strategy as a kind of insurance because you might lose profit on the assets that were already in your possession or even from making a profit on the bear market. If you estimate that the price of the certain stock is going to be lower in the next few months, this can be one of the best strategies for you to consider. Put buying is used very often by those who own stocks and want to lock their selling price. This way the owners protect their money against the potential declinations of the stock. This strategy can also be used to speculate on the stocks on the market that don't belong to you. If you decide to go with the Put buying strategy, you should expect to make a profit only when the value of the stock starts to decrease. At that point premium on the options, you have will rise which will increase your financial return. Even though this strategy can be very useful in down stock markets it can be a substitute strategy for short-selling stocks too.

Covered Call is one more strategy that belongs to the simple strategy group. It is mostly used to write a covered call option and its main characteristic is that is very straightforward. It is based on a premise that you can write (or sell in this case) a Call Option for stock that is already in your possession. Or you can use it to buy new shares in parallel with writing the call. This type of purchase is otherwise known as a buy-write strategy. If someone gives you a premium in advance for the option you wrote your only concern should be if the option will be exercised or not.

The ideal solution for you would be that the option is never exercised. The investors mostly chose this strategy if they have a generation of additional profit in mind. This is especially useful on stocks that according to them won't have an increase in value, at least not in the next few months, so the covered calls are actually replacing dividends for their stock. The main risk of the Covered Call strategy is the possibility of exercising the option. If the investor who bought the option from you exercise it, you have to be able to cover the money you received by selling some of your stocks.

Still, if the stock increases in value, there is a way to protect your premiums by purchasing Call Option that has the same characteristics as the one you sold and to close out your position on that matter. The premium that you have to pay for this kind of action should be similar to the amount of cash you received for the Call Option you wrote and sold to the other investor.

Married Put is a strategy that enables you to purchase a Put Option for the stock that you previously obtained. Also, using this strategy you gain the possibility of buying both the stock and the Put Option for it at the same time. As an options trader, you would consider this strategy if you want to protect your investment from loss in case the value of the stock starts decreasing dramatically for some reason. Married Put is a simple technique that in reality has the role of insurance police for trading options.

A spread, on the other hand, is another strategy from the simple group and it involves two types of transactions. These transactions are simultaneously executed under the normal conditions of the trade. Some experts say that spreads represent a bit advanced strategy comparing to the others mentioned above. However, for someone who is just starting, the simplest methods the better results. Spreads, as our next reviewed strategy (we will talk more about it in some of the following chapters), has a common type that is widely used. These spreads are known as the vertical spreads.

Vertical spreads mean that two options in comparison have different strike prices. When it comes to spreading transactions, each one has named a leg and it comes with a benefit that is one of the main reasons why investors love using spread as their main strategy. One of the best features of spread is the fact that investor's risk of the potential loss of premiums and investment in total is reduced to a minimum. However, this means that the profit that one can gain is limited too, which is why this is considered to be one of the main disadvantages of the spreads.

There are several kinds of vertical spreads. One of them is called a Bull Call Spread, and it is a spread that is mostly used by those who are considered to be bullish purchasers. This means that the purchaser would get stock and a Call Option on it for a strike price that is placed at the current market and at the same time he would sell a Call Option on this same stock that he has but for a higher strike price. In this case, both options in trade would have the same date of expiration.

Another kind of vertical spread that we meet often is the one called Bear Put Spread. In this strategy, the investor obtains Put Options rather than Call Options, also at the strike price that is currently on the market and he simultaneously sells the same amount of Put Options but for a strike price that is significantly lower than the original one. The condition is that all Puts have to be connected to the same underlying stock that has the investor and they must have the same date of expiration. This type of strategy is most frequently used by bearish investors as a substitute for short-selling their stocks because they estimated that the value of the stock will go down.

A few more spread strategies can appear while trading. One of them is Bear Put Spread, which also belongs to vertical spreads we previously explained. Bear Put Spread is used for buying Put Options for the current strike price and as before, at the same time sell the same amount of Put Options for the strike price that is lower than the original one. It is, in fact, the same as with the Call Options in terms of being connected to the same underlying stock and the same expiration date. Bear Put Spread is mostly used as a substitute for short-selling stocks if the option holder predicts that the price of its stock is going to go lower.

The butterfly spread is a strategy that is more complicated than the other ones, and it is not recommended for those who are inexperienced in trading. The reason for this is the fact that the option holder has to combine more simple strategies, or in this particular case bear and bull spread. The main characteristic of this strategy is that it uses three strike prices and all of them are different which is why beginners shouldn't consider this method until they are really confident in their skills. However, it is useful to be familiar with more complex strategies, which is why we will review some of them too, and later give some concrete examples.

Straddle or otherwise known as Long, is a strategy that investors turn to if they believe that there are going to be some big changes on the market and the price of the stock is going to move drastically, but they can't say for sure if the price is going up or down. Straddle allows them to sell or buy both types of options (Call and Put) for the stock. However, the purchase of these options has to be done at the same strike price and they both need to have the same date of expiration. This way investor is offered unlimited potential for gaining profit and risk at the same time.

One of the most complex strategies for option trading is called Iron Condor. It combines short and long positions that an investor has to obtain and hold simultaneously by using two distinct strangle methods. Iron Condor enables the investor to sell Put Options that are labeled as ''out of the money'' and to buy other Put Options labeled the same way but at a different lower strike price. Furthermore, the investor can sell not only Put Options but Call Options too, and it works at the same principle of selling those which are labeled as ''out of the money'' Call Options and buy other ones which have a larger strike price. This strategy is very useful for people who want to limit the risk of their investments and have a high probability of making a profit even though it usually isn't very big.

Iron Butterfly represents another very complex strategy. Iron Butterfly combines limited profit and risk to protect the investment. This strategy is based on the premise that the investor will purchase a Put Option that is seen as ''out of the money'', it further requires that he or she sells a Put Option that is ''at the money'' while selling ''at the money'' Call Option at the same time and purchasing another Call Option but labeled as '' out of the money''.

When it comes to risky strategies, one classic example is the one known as ''Naked Calls''. With this highly risky method investor has the possibility of writing Call Options using the underlying security of that option without actual ownership on it. The risk is high because the person who purchases that option can exercise it in which case the investor (in this case a person who wrote the Call Option) must purchase stock to meet the order and it has to be bought by the current market price. If this scenario happens, the risk is unlimited because it is impossible to predict the price for that stock on the market.

Collars or the Protective strategy is one in which the investor can buy a Put Option that is ''out of the money'', and at the same time, he can write Call Option that is considered to be ''out of money'' too. The same principle on the expiration date and stock is the same for both types of options applies here too. Collars are proven to be very useful if the trader doesn't want to sell the stock but wants to lock in his or her profit.

Strangle or the Long strategy, is the one in which the investor has the opportunity to buy Call Option and Put Option together. In most of the cases, both types that the trader purchases are ''out of the money'' and both options must have the same date of expiration and connection to the same stock. The difference is that their strike prices aren't the same. Many people consider this strategy if they are not sure if their stock is going to increase or decrease in value.

Strategies you can use based on the outlook of the market
Many strategies can be used depending on the goals you want to achieve or the level of the skill that you have. Still, it is significant that you know which strategy is useful regardless of your choice of observing just marketing outlook or focusing on certain security when considering the method. In the following section, we will list strategies based on this outlook. As you will see, they are also categorized as neutral ones, bull strategies, bear market strategies, exit strategies and so forth.

Neutral Strategies are Calendar Spread, Butterfly Spreads, Married Put, Collar, Straddle, Iron Condor, Strangle, etc.

When it comes to Bulls strategies, we have Married Put, Collar, Long Call, Short Put, Bull Put Spread, Covered Call, and Bull Call Spread.

Bear strategies, however, include the following: Naked Call, Bear Put Spread, Short Call, Bear Call Spread, and Long Put.

Exit Strategies

Having an exit strategy is a vital part of any successful investment. You must develop this strategy before you begin options trading. This way you will avoid losses that can are unnecessary. An exit strategy can be used at any point in time as long as it is within the time frame of the duration of the option. It means that once the expiration date has passed you close your position or exit it anymore. Having the right timing to exit the contract is the key to either make money or lose it. That is why you should think about closing your position in case of having options that are ''out of the money' 'in the money'' or ''at the money''.

One of the methods you can use as an exit strategy is to close out your option. You can do that in two ways: you can sell the option that you bought earlier or you can buy the option that you sold before. This means that you actually just need to reverse your position. In case the premium for the option has increased in the meantime you will gain profit. However, if the premium value is lower at the moment you would want to sell the option and that way avoids the potential loss of the money.

When you are a writer of options most of the time you don't need to meet the requirement of buying the underlying security. The reason for this is the fact that you are not able to even close your position unless the option is being exercised. Even in this kind of situation, good timing is a decisive factor. We can say that timing is the single most important factor in options trading which is why you must always carefully track your investment and estimate the right time to sell or buy options to cut losses or take deserved profits. The volatilities of the options become more intense as the date of expiration approaches, which is why you need to keep a close eye on them.

Another exit strategy that you might take into consideration is known as Rolling Out. In case you are not willing to close your position on the options, there is another solution- you can roll them. This strategy combines closing and opening positions. First of all, you need to close out the existing position and then to open new ones. Keep in mind that these newly opened positions have to be identical to the ones you have sold. The only difference is that they should have a different strike price and new expiration date (in an ideal scenario you should have both, but more frequently traders can obtain only one of these two things).

If you don't like the concept of the previous two exit strategies there is another one. Exercising options is a method that is used by holders that want to buy underlying security and they estimate that there will be a need for exercising. The only reasonable moment in which a holder chooses to use this strategy is when his or her options are ''in the money'' because if the options are labeled as the other two categories it would be senseless to do so. When it comes to option writers, they don't have any control over the buyer's decision to exercise the option or not.

When you analyze all scenarios that can happen while trading and you decide what exit strategy will best suit you, you have to keep monitoring your position at any moment and you have to be persistent in following through the goals that you have set and the strategies that you decided to use to make that happen. Trading options come at a fast pace and it is easy for the person to get caught up in the short-term gain and lose the goals that were set long-term. One of the unwritten rules in any trade is that you mustn't allow your emotion to overpower you. You need to stick to the plan you have prepared because, at the end of the day, you have put time, knowledge, effort and money into making the best possible path to make a profit with long-term goals in mind.

Chapter 5

Good Resources and Their Importance in Option Trading

Every successful investor says that research makes all the difference not only in options trading but trading in general. The better resources you have the more knowledge you will acquire. This is especially significant for learning as much as you can about underlying securities for example or to find as many details about the market that is constantly changing. Significance of the right source of information eventually becomes the key to your progress, even more, if the world of options trading is still new to you. We can say that there are two types of relevant resources for options trading. The first one includes traditional resources such as magazines, newsletters, and newspapers. The second type is newer, it has a variety of options and these kinds of resources are mostly referred to as online resources.

The Internet offers a variety of free content, which is why many investors see it as their first stop whenever they need some kind of information. Further technology development also had a huge impact on the amount of information, tools, and possibilities that a person can access so using apps for education and trading, in general, has become a common thing. In the following text, we will list some of the most relevant option trading resources divided into the categories we explained above.

Even though they are considered to be more traditional, magazines, newspapers, newsletters, are still popular for research, for both experienced investors and beginners on the market. It is useful to know that many newsletters offer paid services such as recommendations, picks, research of certain categories and other relevant information.

We will start with the magazines. Some of them such as Forbes is still one of the greatest and strongest magazines in the world for this matter. So we have Fortune, Forbes, Consumer Money Adviser, Bloomberg BusinessWeek, Kiplinger's, and Fast Company as some of the most relevant magazines today.

Newspapers that you might find useful are: the Financial Times, the Wall Street Journal, The Washington Post, Value Line, and Barron's.

As we already mentioned, newsletters often offer more detailed insight into the market matters. Some of the most recommended ones are: ETF Trader, Market Watch Options Trader, The Proactive Fund Investor, Hulbert Interactive, The Technical Indicator, The Prudent Speculator, Dow Theory Forecasts, and Global Resources Trading

When it comes to online resources, they are probably the most frequent source of information for everything, not only for options trading. However, it is possible to find numerous websites that offer research that is up to date. Many of these analyses and other useful data can be found for free. Here are some of the best-graded sites for you to start: the Wall Street Journal, MarketWatch.com, Bloomberg.com, Morningstar.com, Financial Times, TheStreet.com, The Motley Fool, BigCharts.com, MSN Money/CNBC, YCHARTS.com, Yahoo!Finance.com, and so forth.

Technology development made many things easier with trading. Many apps have emerged and enabled investors to keep a close track of their investments at all times. It is important to know that there are apps that are not only for investment but for brokerage companies too. In the following text, you can find some of the investment apps that are most frequently used and that have excellent feedback. Some of them are CNN Money, SigFig, Stock Twits, Personal Capital, Bloomberg, Motif Investing, Stock of the Day, and Yahoo! Finance app.

How to avoid costly mistakes

Losing profit is not something that you want as an investor since the main purpose of options trading is to make money not the other way around. To do so, some tips can help you avoid mistakes that can be costly.

First of all, don't invest more capital than you are ready to lose. Keep in mind that trading options don't go without risks. There aren't any guarantees that the propositions that you'll face with will gain you anything and your decisions are based on the hunch. Furthermore, if you don't have good timing and your hunch isn't right, you can lose the entire investment, not only the cash you were expecting to earn. The best way to avoid this kind of scenario is to start small. It is recommended that you use no more than 15 percent of your total portfolio on options trading.

The second tip that you should be aware of at all times is that good research gets the job done. If somebody says that it is a good idea to invest in options and you rush in and make an order without thinking it through, once more, you can lose more than you could earn. You should make your own research and make a decision based on facts before you start trading.

There is another thing that you should be mindful of. No matter the strategy you choose for options trading, you should always try to adjust it to the current condition on the market. Not all strategies work in all environments which is why you must be up to date with circumstances in the world of finance and you have to adapt accordingly.

Without a proper exit strategy, it is useless to talk about successful business in options trading. You need to make a plan that you will follow through regardless of your emotions. Rational decisions are the main factor in trade, being emotional and making fast decisions out of rage or spite or feeling of insecurity can only make things worse. Stick to the plan you figured before you started trading because it should have both downside and upside points along with the timeframe for its execution. Just like you shouldn't let negative feelings influence your decision making, you shouldn't allow the feeling of over-confidence in gaining large profits pull you back from the path you have set for yourself.

When it comes to risks, there is no need to take more risks than necessary, which means that the level of risk should be as big as your comfort with it. Level of risk tolerance is different for everyone, it is an individual think and only the investor himself can set its limit. Try to estimate that level and then choose all further actions accordingly. It is the safest premise to base your decisions on without being too insecure about every choice you make.

Chapter 6

Technical Analysis and Its Basics

No matter the kind of vehicle you choose for your actions, there are some basics that you have to be familiar with. This fundamental knowledge is mostly connected to the behavior of the markets. If you learn how to recognize the way they behave, you will be able to anticipate the movement of the prices more accurately, thus make smarter decisions while trading. It can be interesting to note that regardless of the value that is traded on the market, some concepts can always apply to the prices and their way of performance on the market.

This can be explained by independent traders and investors being responsible for short-term price fluctuations. We can say that the price depends on the actions of the people who invest or trade values on the market and that prices react in a similar way when they are given similar input or stimuli. The study that is dedicated to researching the ways of price behavior is called technical analysis and understanding its basic is one of the most essential education points that you will need to be able to make correct financial decisions on the market.

The basics of Technical Analysis

Technical analysis represents a huge topic. If you decide to enter the market and become an investor, there is a high possibility that you will catch yourself coming back to studying and learning something new many times for as long as you intend to work as a trader. That is why every person knowledgeable in options trading would advise that a basic understanding of technical analysis is a very important step for every person involved in the market. However, you don't need to know everything about it right away. Since it is a large area of research, it is ok if for some aspects of your business you just research parts of the technical analysis that you are particularly interested in for that concrete project. For instance, the technical analysis offers more than a hundred indicators for analyzing the market. In reality, traders usually use three or four, mostly the most popular ones or just those that they were familiar within the first place.

If you don't limit yourself only to option trading but you do trading in general, you will realize that technical analysis can be applied to any financial instruments such as futures or stocks for example.

We can say that their basis is in psychology and human nature in general and how they behave in practice. For better understanding, we will overview some of the main topics in technical analysis. These topics will be:

Technical analysis' foundation; how to chart principles and trends; patterns in technical analysis; technical analysis through the movement of the averages, and Indicators in technical analysis.

Technical analysis' foundation

The main basis of the technical analysis is found in the term known as '' market action''. Market action represents a whole personal knowledge about the trading market, and it doesn't include information that you might obtain from an insider. It can be simply defined as a study that determines: ''the way that the price moves over time''. If possible, it also examines its volumes and how they change over time too.

Still, the fundamental concept of technical analysis is based on the premise that the behavior of the market is a reflection of everything that happened and will happen with the price at a certain moment. Many things can have an impact on the price, and the amount of the impact depends on the market in which the trade is made. That's where technical analysis comes in, it cuts across all of those possibilities and states that all the things that can be known about the price are basically already included in the price that we see at the moment we want to trade.

This means that you shouldn't worry too much about the things that influence the price, as according to this it is enough to follow how the price changes over time and you will get all your answers. At first, many people wondered if this kind of principle can work because it sounded rather easy. If you had any doubts, the answer was already proven and it says that yes, technical analysis is successful although this kind of definition doesn't seem that complicated.

However, there is one very important point coming out from all of this. Technical analysis doesn't guarantee the behavior of the price. It can tell you that the price will increase or decrease for a certain period, but that doesn't necessarily happen. It may or it may not. The reason for this is that regardless of the calculation that the market has to do something, it is impossible to be 100 percent sure that it will. The market has its own ways and eventually does what it wants. So what technical analysis does is that it gives you the indication that shows what will be the most probable outcome, which means that the only certainty that you get is to know if the law of probability is on your side or not.

You can do a large number of average trades and hopefully make some profit, but you should never invest an amount of money or some valuable goods such as your house or your car if you can't afford to lose it. It is not recommended especially if one successful trade makes you confident that just one is enough to be a good technical indicator for certain gain. This is one of the reasons why the first task of technical analysis is to improve your chance for success by analyzing the prices and the way they behave on the market.

The second reason for the analysis is the fact that prices almost always change using certain trends. For instance, if the price increases its trend will be to rise until there is something that disables it from further growth. In comparison, we can say that prices act like Newton's motion law, which says that: ''a body in motion will stay in motion unless acted upon by an external force.''

Of course, to prove this to be true, it has to happen over time. If this wasn't the case the price charts represented in many analyses wouldn't be the way they are. They would be illustrated as a random movement of the prices. The third reason is that technical analysis supposes that history will, as always, repeat itself. If certain situations happened in the past, and you see them happening once again in the present than it is highly expected that the same thing will happen in the future too. Since people are not expected to change in this equation, the second logical conclusion would be that their results will be the same too. In a nutshell- this was a very foundation of technical analysis. Don't forget that one of the most efficient ways to become good in trading and to increase your chance to become a successful investor is to be able to use most of the things that this analysis can give you.

There are a few arguments that you can hear against the use of technical analysis. Still, the only proof that you really need is the fact that this analysis works and that at least it can improve your chances to get more percentages while trading. However, we will point out some of the attitudes toward technical analysis:

One of the traders said: *"Charts only show what has happened in the past, how they can reveal what hasn't happened yet?"* The answer to this is quite simple, there is evidence from earlier trades and those pieces of evidence are used in technical analysis with the premise that history will repeat itself. This way you can anticipate at least with some fair certainty what is the next thing that will happen with the price on the market. In comparison, it works in a similar way as the weather forecast, if they say that it will rain on the TV, you know that it might not rain even though they said it will, but you take your umbrella with you anyway. The same principle applies with the technical analysis and that is how you can predict the future by using the past events.

Another trader noted: *''If the prices already incorporate everything there is to know, then any change in price can only come from new information that we don't know yet.''* This kind of idea doesn't only appear in trading options, it is present in all financial markets. It surfaces in many areas and even academics are still discussing it. Differently, from the opinion that is popular between the traders, this concept doesn't actually say that the price that is currently on the market is the correct one. It just states that it isn't possible to establish if that current price is too low or too high. That is why the smartest choice to deal with this concept is to prove in which way technical analysis really works. In the end, if everyone supported this kind of idea then we would have zero analysis and the price would be always the same. We can imply that technical analysis has self-fulfilling characteristics.

This means that if the majority of traders do the analysis and estimate that the price has to increase all of them would become buyers on the market, which would mean an increase in demand, thus price that went up. The same principle applies to the price that is supposed to go down. This is one more example in which technical analysis showed that it works. Of course, there can always be some doubts but does it really matter to prove why the price went in the direction that you thought it would? Additionally, if a large number of traders who are not well educated and they just want to make quick profit fail, it can be seen as a sort of evidence that the idea of having a massive amount of traders regardless of their knowledge and dedication is somehow wrong from the beginning.

How to chart principles and trends

After we have seen what the basic principles of the technical analysis are, it is time to see how the prices are charted or graphed and what those graphs mean. There is no way of escaping this even though some might find it unnecessary. You will be forced to see this kind of chart during your whole trading career. It is easier to understand these principles if you go slowly, step by step and try to remember how these principles work. There are few diverse types of the chart but all of them mostly use horizontal bottom and timescale as a vertical scale.

The price is usually up to the side, and for someone who is just starting, these charts are the only ones that you should be interested in. The vertical line or the timescale can be expressed in minutes, in days, or even weeks, so you will look at the one, which is suitable for your trading style. However, it is not unusual that you'd want to know what happens with the other time scales as long as they are around the values you chose. Experienced traders mostly look at the other time scales to get the bigger picture on what's happening on the market. Here, we will mention three kinds of charts and we will suppose that they all have the same time vertical line and that they are all in the same currency. Once that we accepted this hypothetical conditions we can say that here we will review the line chart, candlestick chart, and the bar chart.

In the first chart, we will talk about, the line chart is the one that has the least amount of information if we compare it to the other two. The only data you can find in this chart is the closing price's plots for certain periods and then these plots and periods are connected with the line. The line chart isn't used very often but it represents the basis for the next two- the candlestick and the bar chart. Even though all three show more or less the same information, traders prefer using the candlestick for instance, because according to them it is easier to understand it immediately when you see it, which is not the case with the rest of the mentioned charts. It is a way of recalling the definition of the ''market action'', which says that market action represents all we know about prices.

If you look at the chart that is known as the candlestick one, you will notice several vertical lines that are referred to like candles. These so-called candles can represent a four-hour chart for example, and the reason for that is the fact that in this period four plotted prices are different for every period in the chart. These prices are known as the highest price, the lowest price, the one that occurs at the beginning of the period (the opening price) and the one that is estimated to be at the end of the period or at the end of that trade (otherwise known as the closing price). Candlestick chart is actually a Japanese method for illustrating clearly this kind of information. However, this chart was used in the West for a few decades.

Before this chart appeared, the traders in the West used just the bar chart because it was the only one available at the time. The cleverness of the candlestick chart is shown through color change for example. The bar charts, on the other hand, use only thin lines, which we know as tics. These tics have their levels and they show closing prices and opening prices with these small tics. Contrarily, candles in the candlestick chart show you the difference in price by changing its color. The color depends on the value of the price for that day, and the change in color occurs with the price going up and down accordingly.

This way it is much easier to spot the changes in the chars. The common colors that are used in these charts are black and white. As you can already assume if the candle body is white the price will go up, and if it's black, the price is going down. Nowadays, technology is more improved, so there are options to put the colors that you like. The only criteria that matter is that you can immediately recognize if there are some changes in the market and if the price you were interested in ended uprising or falling.

When it comes to trends, the fundamental idea of trends is to indicate if the price will go up or down in general. Trends on the market are happening for about 40 percent of the time, on average. The rest of the time trends float around the same percentage and that kind of floating is known as moving ''sideways'', or range trading if you prefer. There are diverse strategies that can be useful if applied following the behavior of the market. For easier understanding, we will not go with the standard definitions of uptrends and downtrends. We will just say that the uptrend means that the price is going high and reaching even higher peaks but its point is low.

Contrarily, downtrend means that once that the points start going lower the next logical thing is that the price will tend to reach its lower peaks. As you can now assume, the trend doesn't mean that the prices will go only straight up or straight down. The prices don't do that, they wiggle around instead. Since trends are one of the most significant indicators of technical analysis, you must be very careful and try not to rely on the definition itself. Your point of view also has an influence on this matter. For example, let's say that you have a chart with a larger time frame in which we now see a simple uptrend. However, if you divide those uptrends into smaller periods you can see few smaller uptrends but this time they are interspersed with some small downtrends which are why you should observe your trends carefully especially the periods in which your trade should be over.

When a price acts reluctantly and it refuses to go beyond a certain level it means that we are talking about support and resistance. Support represents a level of price that is lower than the market one. If by any chance current price goes below that level it can happen that it will go back up or reverse in the process.

Resistance is a level of price that is higher than the level of the current price. This means that if the current price goes over this level there is a high probability that will go back down. Some traders describe the role of the support and resistance levels as a kind of magic. These levels act like borders and they are quite resistant.

Some of the basic points of these "borders" say that the more times that the price hits either the support or resistance level and bounces back, the more you should base your estimations on those reactions. Also, going back further in time and finding the similar or even the same levels means that these levels are even stronger, thus more reliable. If by some chance current price penetrates one of these two levels then they will just reverse their role. For example, if the price breaks the resistance then it is highly probable that when it starts going down it will stop at that level using resistance as its support.

In traditional definitions, resistance and support are considered to be actual prices of the asset or the set level. They were also always expressed as whole numbers such as 20, 50, 1.000 or some other number that looks significant for example.

There is one more type of resistance and support levels otherwise known as the "channel line" and the "trend line". It is said that the trend line in an uptrend is sloping. This means that this level slopes upward and it has a successive increase in the bottom of the prices that are connected. On the other hand, we have a channel line which is sloping down and it has successively falling peaks on the market that are also connected. The trend line is usually drawn as the parallel line to the channel one and they are always drawn one the different (opposite) sides of the particular price. If we imagine a chart that shows an uptrend, the trend line, in this case, would be the bottom line and it will connect the bottoms and the troughs of the price on that chart. On the contrary, the channel line would be the line that is drawn up, but still parallel to the trend line. There has to be enough space between the lines so they can connect their peaks without crossing. In this case, this channel is the one that shows the behavior of support and resistance levels of the price that can change over time. If we say that in our candlestick chart there is one candle that is lower than the trend line than that is the kind of information that we should focus on and determine our further decisions accordingly. Remember that none of this is set in stone and it can easily change.

Prices can change rapidly and it can happen that you will find them below trend line, which will mark the end of one trend, and then the price will just enter the range trading or perhaps a downtrend too. However, keeping an eye on this kind of changes can influence significantly on your further trading.

Patterns in technical analysis

When we talk about charts, in this section we will review the general shapes of those that are graphed in the price lines. We would point out that these kinds of shapes are characteristic of traditional technical analysis in the West. Some other sections will have more details about patterns on candlestick charts in which the appearance of a few candles represents a separate pattern.

Reversal Patterns are the patterns that indicate that it is imminent that the trend will become reversible. These patterns are often used in options trading because once when you establish that the price is going to reverse its direction, it is easy for you to make the right move and make a good profit.

Head and Shoulders are one of the patterns that every student in financial trading is familiar with. This pattern is considered to be one of the most reliable patterns when we talk about Western style. Head and Shoulders are built up out of the three peaks on the market in which the middle peak represents the head while the other two adjacent peaks represent shoulders. This pattern is in an uptrend by default and it suggests when the price will reverse and go into its downtrend. If we imagine a chart that shows a reversal pattern of head and shoulders, we would see that we can draw a trend line that can complete the channel of the price. However, this channel line wouldn't work if some of the prices went above it, but in case they don't, this chart is applicable. Keep in mind that charts can't be copied all of the time, every chart represents a different price case and different points in time on the market.

Still, if you use head and shoulders, you can use a line that is drawn across the shoulders and it will represent a so-called neckline. Drawing a neckline has few points now. First of all, shoulders are always below the head but when it comes to just shoulders, it is not important which one is above the other. We can use the neckline for sloping up like in our case. We can say that the head and shoulder pattern is confirmed if the price goes from the head down through the neckline, If you put some thoughts into it you will see that this pattern isn't that complicated, it just has an uptrend description that flatters the image a trader would want to see on the price chart.

Inverse Head and Shoulders is actually a regular Head and Shoulders chart just turned upside down. This way you can see the end of the downtrend of the price and knowing that you can assume when the uptrend of the price will start. All other characteristics are the same as with the regular pattern.

Double and Triple Tops and Bottoms are a kind of pattern that also has similarities with the head and shoulders. However, as their name suggests, they have two or three peaks, and not the ''head'' that is the highest point on the chart. Generally speaking, if the trend doesn't have any progress and the peaks don't rise up to the levels they previously did, we can conclude that the trend is weaker. Contrarily, we can recognize the reversed trend once when we see that the price is heading back down which is somewhat common sense if we take everything we already learned in the previous chapters.

Continuation Patterns are the patterns that just happen and once they do, the price goes in its previous direction. Continuation patterns are considered to be in effect if the consolidation appears before the further price push.

Triangles are the patterns that can provide a good insight into the progress of the price paths. In most cases, triangles serve to narrow the time and to squeeze the range of the price up to the point that I can't be contained anymore so it has to break out. This way you get more direct indications if there is going to be any dramatic change in the way that the price moves. For example, let's say that the triangle is ascending. This kind of triangle usually appears if the price is in an uptrend and it shows that the same price as it approaches its resistance level while being constantly rebuffed.

Ultimately, the rebuffing continues until the price breaks through. It means that you are actually looking at the price that goes from one converging trend line to another until it breaks out somewhere between the way along the triangle. To better understand the factors that influenced the behavior of the price you should be aware of the fact that buyers are the key factors that are pushing the price. They repeat and repeat their pushes until the sellers take over and let the price drop. So, we can say that buyers are those who push the price up until it reaches its resistance level. When that happens sellers awaken and push the price back down which eventually leads to break out of the price that now goes upwards. As usual, there is always an opposite pattern so you can apply similar principles to the descending triangle. As its name suggests, this triangle shows a downtrend of the price.

We'd like to point out that these examples don't necessarily mean that these two triangles can't appear in opposite trends which mean that it isn't imperative to say that the price can only go up if the ascending triangle appears or that it can only go down in case you have a descending triangle. The thing is that in most cases this is likely to be the configuration of the pattern. Reversed criteria for triangles occur rarely which is why ones that we described above are considered to be the default ones. However, it can also happen that you get a symmetrical triangle. In that case, the upper line will be sloping down and the lower line will be sloping up. Symmetrical triangles are often referred to as the pausing points for the trend that is observed. After this pause, the trend continues going in its direction whether it is a downtrend or an uptrend.

The main feature of all triangles mentioned above is that at one point the price has to be resolved. Otherwise, the price range will continue oscillating and its range will start to shrink. When the price breaks out you can have a good idea in which direction will head to once it leaves the triangle.

Last but not the least type of the triangle we will mention is known as the broadening formation. It is the one that is different from the rest of the triangle patterns we reviewed. Another name for this pattern is the megaphone top. The main characteristic of this triangle is that the lines of the trend are opened outwards or they just broaden as time goes by. This type of triangle represents a chaotic state on the market, which usually means that the prices are going wild and that oscillation in their value is big and unpredictable. If you happen to see this kind of pattern while trading, it is most likely that the price will be in an uptrend that is followed by the downtrend, even so, you should reconsider taking any action in that kind of situation because the risk levels are enormous until the market becomes stable again.

The flag and the rectangle are patterns that have similar characteristics. They are both the indicators that show how much the price oscillates once we place it between two parallel lines. If the flag pattern is in an uptrend it means that in most of the cases it will be the same as the continuation pattern even though there are some exceptions, like with all trades in general. The flag has one distinctive thread, they usually show up after a sharp move that someone did and it's like the whole market needs to process that event. In the meantime, most often that period lasts for a few weeks, consolidating happens, and afterward, the previous trend continues. In most of the cases, the flag appears and slopes around a countertrend.

Technical analysis through the movement of the averages

One of the most frequently used indicators in technical analysis and trading, in general, is an indicator called the moving average. It is also considered to be one of the most versatile ones. Movement of the averages can be used in a few different ways and they are understandable which makes them very suitable and popular when it comes to tools needed for making an analysis. The main difference between these patterns and patterns of recognition is the fact that you don't need to interpret the meaning of the moving average. It is unambiguous and it can be tested using any information that is historically recorded on the trading systems you use.

Most people know what an average means and how to calculate it. Just to make sure that we are on the same page we will go through this simple process: firstly you take a certain number and add them together, then you divide them by this X that you have and you get the average number that you needed. So if we take numbers one, three, six, and eight for example and add them we will have 1+3+6+8. Then we divide this number by four and we get the number that is considered to be an average. When it comes to trading, calculating the movement of an average is done the same way in which X represents the value of the price up until today and including its value at the moment.

Simple Moving Average (SMA)

So an SMA or Simple Moving Average, as its name suggests, takes the price from the last five trades and get the value of the current price. Every trading session has its own simple moving average and they are all connected in a way that illustrates the form of the continuous chart. Let's see an example of a simple moving average: We will take that the SMA is 14, which means that we will add up 14 previous prices and their averages for every trading period.

The way that this kind of chart is made indicates that there are lags inactions of the price and that the price is acting like it was playing ''catch-up'' game most of the time. Generally speaking, this lag is better known as a ''lag-ging'' indicator. This lag has a role to smoothen out the action of the price and to show the trader the direction in which the trend will develop further. As a matter of fact, the value of the simple moving average has few tendencies, and it can be represented as a curving line of the trend thus marking out the levels of support and resistance. If the value of the price goes lower, the simple moving average line fill is closer to the price, following it; and when the value becomes large the simple moving average tends to smooth out the information from the price.

Exponential Moving Average (EMA)

This pattern is different yet very similar to the simple moving average. When it comes to the exponential moving average, it is important to know that it was invented with a purpose to eliminate as much of the time lag as possible. It was believed that that way the line would become more relevant and that it would represent a more accurate current price.

Other than these, we can say that there are many others "moving average" patterns that are used in technical analysis. Some of them are triangular moving average, the weighted moving average, the variable moving average, and so forth. All of these averages use their own unique methods that combine prices that were used in previous trading periods to calculate the current price as correctly as possible so they can make better projections for the future trades.

Single Moving Average

This average pattern is considered to be one of the simplest methods that a trader can use to predict when to do the trade. A single moving average can be taken as a signal that shows when the price crossed the moving average that you plotted on your chart. If the moving average is older than the price that crossed it, that price is bullish, if however, the recent price goes lower than the moving average it means that the price is bearish.

There are a few different kinds of these averages in terms of periods and numbers. The most obvious trade to make while using the chart is to wait for the price to drop below one-quarter of the moving average point. When the price reaches the middle of the chart that usually means that the price will go up. In this case, the trade would qualify as the long one or it can just stand still and go neither up nor down. If the price manages to increase its value by going through the single moving average two more times, it means that you are making a profit. Your actions depend on the way you want to close your current trades.

If you choose to wait until the price crosses the single moving average more than once you can also lose gains, not only earn them. There are, however, exit strategies that can be applied in these kinds of situations. If you are a beginner, you can use the system and refine it by playing with numbers and see what outcomes you will get. The more possibilities you can spot, the more prepared you become for the actual decision when the time comes.

Two Moving Averages

In technical analysis, there are many ways to search for a signal that will let you know when it is the best time to trade. One of those ways when it comes to moving averages is to plot two of them. Each of the two moving averages should be based on a different period. In this situation, the best moment for you to start trading is to wait for these moving averages to cross one another. More or less it is a similar concept to the one of the above, just smoother.

In the end, even the current price in this scenario is actually a variation of one hypothetical single moving average. The most frequently used pairs in plotting two moving averages include numbers such as a 10 and a 25, or a 20 and a 100, and so forth, and it is a matter of a personal preference on which way you will combine these numbers and what will be the best solution for you. Let's say that you use plot numbers 5 and 20 for your two moving averages.

If we imagine a chart, we can say that by the left edge both averages will cross their paths and it will mean that you are in for a long trade. Afterward, the averages cross their paths again, now that happened on the quarter of the way and this time it meant that the short trade will begin. When the averages cross in the middle the long trade will begin again, and so on. If we look again in this example, we can see that this pattern works quite well even though that the trader has to wait for the averages to cross back before he or she can close their trades. Again, there is always a possibility of trying different kinds of numbers and having different moving averages thus experiencing different performances that are followed with diverse decision making. With these crossings of the moving averages, the unambiguous signal becomes perfectly clear and you immediately recognize when the right time for you to start the trade is. The main advantage of this method is that it can be used consistently.

Bollinger Bands

Bollinger Bands are a refined version of moving averages. Like all of the other patterns, they also can have a few different uses. Bollinger bands represent a plot of three lines. The line in the center represents a moving average while the other two are spaced from the main one depending on the volatility of the price. These two lines that are spaced from the central one as one above and the one below are often referred to as two standard deviations. Deviation, in this case, has the same meaning as the deviations in statistics.

The meaning of this is that these two lines will go further apart or they will get tighter. It all depends on the fluctuation of the price. If we imagine our simple chart again, we can say that these lines referred to as two deviations are actually trying to contain the current price, and they open up only if the price moves a lot, but as soon as the price becomes steady, they close upon it. According to the statisticians, these two standard deviations actually contain around 95 percent of the total movement of the price. The most common behavior of the price is to follow the band, but it rarely happens that the price penetrates it.

If the band acts as a support source on the left side of our chart we can say that this happens on the downtrend part of the illustration. Then on the right side of that chart, we will have erratic movements of the price but it would still just hit the resistance level and that will be done repeatedly whenever the price reaches the upper band on the right side. Some traders will see this as a change in trend, which in this case means that the price crossed the middle line

79

making the opposite band be the target of the price. Of course, the middle line here acts as both resistance and support to the price movement. In other words, being in an uptrend means that the price will most likely oscillate between the upper band and the middle band while being in the downtrend means that the price will fluctuate between the lower band and the middle band instead. If the price strayed away significantly from these guidelines than the most probable cause for that is the change of the trend. In case you note that the distance between the bands is narrowing down it means that the Bollinger Band tries to show that the price is about to start a new trend and break out. In comparison, it is a process similar to throttling the price down up to the point where it can't be contained any more at all.

Indicators in technical analysis

Many traders start to feel excited about trading, even more, when they realize that there are many ways to anticipate, at least up to a certain point, where will the price go and then make some profitable trades using these estimations. However, if you are still in your early stages when it comes to option trading, you shouldn't let enthusiasm to take over at least not until you see through everything that is coming your way. In this section, we will discuss indicators that represent values or the lines calculated using the price actions as its basis. Indicators can also be used to provide an insight into the future movement of the prices and overall market sentiment.

There is a large number of indicators and the amount is always rising since new indicators can emerge every time that someone overcomes a shortcoming of those, which we already use. Usually, traders tend to use only a few of them (mostly just two or three) and the fact is that when you want to do estimation for one day or on a day to day basis it is unnecessary to use too many indicators. In this overview, we will talk about oscillators or the indicator, which the main character is to go between two established limits. Oscillation shows the investor if the market that he trades on is overbought or oversold.

The theory behind it says that if the market is oversold it means that too many traders sold out its assets and that the next step needs to be buying back these assets when those who oversold think about their actions. Speaking in terms of pricing, this directly implies that the prices on the market are below the limit. Contrarily, if the market happens to be overbought, it means that traders were too enthusiastic and they rushed into buying stocks. This way they pushed the price too hard. This over push also means that the price will go back down soon enough. In practice, oscillators are usually plotted beneath the chart and separately. We can describe the derivation of this indicator but in reality, the computer takes care of plotting and placing it into the relevant position on the chart. Still, it is good to know from where indicators have all this information along with figuring out when you should use another indicator that will confirm if the signal is ok or you should make another estimation and base it on different criteria.

Moving Average Convergence Divergence (MACD)

Even though it might seem more complicated than the rest of the oscillators that can be seen later, we will start with this one because it is tightly connected to the moving averages. Moving average Convergence Divergence indicator is often used in practice. To be easier to remember, MACD is frequently pronounced as '' mac dee''. MACD can be also shown in regular charts and its position is usually plotted below the regular chart illustration.

The initial step for MACD is to plot the difference between the patterns known as two exponential moving averages (EMA). Keep in mind that the values of exponential moving averages vary and that it depends on the current prices on the market. The value of the difference between these two values can be pointed out with the bars on the indicator below the chart. As we mentioned in previous sections, if the moving averages cross, that means that we received a signal to start our trade by buying or selling on the market.

The most usual tendency during this process is the appearance of the lag, which is usually behind the action of the price. MACD is an indicator plot out the different meaning that when you get zero it is basically the same as the crossing line of two exponential moving averages. At the moment, MACD is just another way of viewing the same thing that we explained before. Still, the signal that we should listen to in this case is actually a plot of moving averages but on MACD value. This way we have the chance to find out in what ways two original exponential moving averages diverge and converge. It also means that through this indicator we can estimate the time of conversion or the time of crossing, thus providing a better and faster signal for the next time. There are a few very significant information that you can obtain from an indicator such as MACD. First of all, if the signal goes lower than the bars on your chart, you can use it as a signal to buy, and also when this signal goes beyond the MACD bars it means that it is time for you to sell. Since the MACD indicator can show tendencies that are both below and above zero, it means that this indicator behaves as an oscillator that shows conditions in which the particular market is oversold or overbought. When MACD reaches a number much higher than zero it means that the market is overbought and that it will be the right time to sell. Contrarily if MACD goes deeply under zero it means that the market is oversold and that it can be the right time to start buying.

Relative Strength Index (RSI)

One of the indicators popular among traders is certainly the relative strength index. This index was used for the first time in more than three decades ago. This indicator analyzes the performances of the price in the predetermined number of periods in the past. Furthermore, the relative strength index compares the number of down days and up days and then sets the main idea about the moment in which the market will go in either uptrend or downtrend direction.

In practice, if the relative strength index is below 30 percent and then it comes back up, this should be understood as a signal to buy options. Contrarily, if the relative strength index is more than 70%

and it goes lower than that it is, in fact, a signal to sell your option. The signal is the moment in which the price gets to be the closest to the middle of the chart not when it hits that level.

Stochastic Oscillator

The stochastic oscillator is an indicator that was invented in the 1990s by Dr. Lane. The interesting fact is that this oscillator was used only by traders and the reason for that was its high effectiveness. Some say that the main cause for that is the fact that a stochastic oscillator pays more attention to the action of the price. This means that the oscillator observes the closing price and its relation to the overall price range for the selected time frame. In other words, if the price is in an uptrend, you can expect that the closing price will never come nearly to the top of the predicted range and if we talk about the downtrends, the closing price will never go near the bottom line. One of the many interesting things about this indicator is the fact that Dr. Lane was experimenting a lot and with many other indicators that were available at the time. It is also interesting to know that this is the main historical reason why most of the lines have strange names, especially the dotted ones. Using its simplest form, the bullish signal in this oscillator can be recognized if the solid line crosses the dotted line. If however the solid line goes through the dotted line and goes down, it means that the signal is bearish. Usually, you only need to wait until the lines are way too much into each other's territory which in percentages would be more than 80 percent for uptrend and lower than 20 percent for a downtrend.

The stochastic oscillator is multiple times more active indicator than the RSI. Still, it can send far too many signals, which means that there is still a risk of trading too frequently. In practice, it is not uncommon to see the traders using both RSI and Lane's oscillator. It is a good combination because the RSI tends to be less volatile and it can make a balance in combination with the indicator that might end up triggering too many trades.

Indicator Use

Many charting programs offer way more indicators than we could possibly discuss in this guide. The ones that we reviewed, however, can be found on the charting program called MetaTrader 4. Regardless of the program or the platform you use, definitions and interpretations are mostly the same. The main function of an oscillator is to give you a warning, or an early signal that the change is about to happen and that appearance of the extreme values in price can mean that the value needs a correction, and the main indicator of this is if the price starts going towards the center. Oscillators have values that can go either lower or higher for the time frame and the price action usually has no change. One more thing to consider about the oscillators is that they are usually just mirroring the real price value and every time that their directions are not the same the price acts like it is being out of the time and the changes can occur.

Chapter 7

Candlestick Charts and Patterns

Candlestick charts weren't known in the West before the 1980s when they were introduced for the first time. However, Japan used this method for centuries, which at the same time makes Japan the place of origin of the candlestick method. As we already have seen before, these charts show basically the same information as the bar chart that was used in our countries way before we started using the Japanese system. The reason that the candlestick charts became so popular in such a short amount of time is the fact that it is easier to understand and it uses simple yet innovative body illustration that helps the investor seeing every change at a glance.

Let's recap some of the basic characteristics of the candlestick as the general pattern. Firstly, the total length of the candle represents the trading range for the predetermined period. The body of the candle is connected to the distance between the prices known as the closing price and the opening price. The difference in color shows if the price went up or down for a certain period. The length of the candle also portrays the volatility of the price and the sum of the candle and the ''body'' of the candle can be viewed as the progress that was made for one day. If the chart shows that the candle's ''body'' is short, it means that the closing and the opening prices were close or similar. If that is the case, we can say that the buyers and the sellers were in balance. Contrarily, the long candle ''body'' means that one side is stronger than the other and that it decisively pushes the price in the direction that suits them.

Types

When it comes to the candlestick chart, we can say that there are regular candles and then that there is Doji. Doji is a special candle which body is just a horizontal line. This line represents closing prices and opening prices, which in case you have Doji are equivalent. Traders from Japan consider Doji as a very important indicator because it represents a balance between those who buy and those who sell on the market. Also, this kind of balance often leads to the conclusion that the price trend will change, thus reverse. Remember, on the chart, the horizontal line can be placed anywhere on the wick. It doesn't matter if it is the top or the bottom or even in the middle of it. On the other hand, we have regular candles that most frequently have short bodies. If the wicks of the candles are high, we are talking about ''high wave'' candles. The meaning of these candles has similarities with the Doji.

If the candles have long bodies that will indicate that the trend of the price is strong. If your chart has candles without any wicks, it means that you got Marubozu. Marumboza is an indicator that shows that the trades were only made in the range of the opening and closing prices, thus no trade was done outside of that range. This is a very strong indication, which means that the market was strongly pushing the price only in one direction. Patterns on the candlestick charts can be made out of one or more candles. These patterns mostly show a reversal even though that some patterns indicate continuation rather than dramatic change.

If you build your interpretations only on the ideas like longitude of the wicks and strength of the candle bodies etc., it can turn into indecisiveness. That is why you have to be extra considerate and to keep in mind that the interpretation of any chart, indicator or pattern can't be done by copy-pasting previous observations. Interpretation depends very much on things such as the trend of the price before this period and the direction of its trends.

Patterns

Hammer

When it comes to ideal signals, in Hammer that signal is represented with a small body. Its wick should be two times longer than the body regardless of the day being up or down for the price trend. Hammer sometimes signals that the trend of the price will reverse. The way to confirm such an assumption and make it actionable is to wait for the next day and see if the price is going to increase. If the price starts raising it means that your interpretation of trend reversal has been confirmed. This pattern works because of many traders panic, and if the price is down for some time they would sell at any price. If we try to express this situation in the candle chart it means that the wick is going to be pushed down. However, smart investors come in and they buy which pushes the price up once again. These trend reversals can last through the whole day and even keep up happening the next day too.

Hanging Man

The Hanging Man is a pattern that looks the same as the Hammer; the only difference is that it comes in an uptrend. Just like before, we search for a change in the price trend on the following day so we could confirm our estimation of the trend's reversal. The psychology, in this case, is that traders mostly decide to take profits. That way they push the prices down. Still, some of those who are new on the market see this as their chance to buy. That way they push the price back up In any case, this candle is considered to be weak. As a reflection of this pattern, it appears that traders have a hunch that this means that the trend is over so the selling starts to rise again in the next few days.

Inverted Hammer

Once you see the diagrams for the first two candlestick patterns you will realize that the inverted hammer also has similar characteristics. There is also certain psychology behind its signaling and we will briefly explain it: Once the downtrend starts weakening and several traders have second thoughts they start buying in which pushes the prices up. Sellers also come back in the game which means that the price will close down. However, if the price starts increasing during the next day than the conclusion is that the weakness of the trend made buyers buying even more while pushing up the prices and that way the uptrend started.

Shooting Star

The last but not the least in the set of four related candle signals is the pattern known as the Shooting Star comes which comes in an uptrend. Everybody knows that beginners or novices if you prefer, tend to buy on the top. Shooting star demonstrates simply the exuberance that later causes the traders to see the high wick that appears when novices enter the market. The traders who notice this are usually those who appeared thinking that it is time to sell. Just like in every other pattern above, the only way to confirm this is to wait up the next day and to determine if that was really the signal that shows that the trend will reverse.

Bullish Engulfing

This is a pattern that consists of two candles and it is graded as highly probable. When in a downtrend, the first candle pressures that the selling continues. The pressure is strong enough to allow the next candle to open up at an even lower price. But those investors who are smart see an opportunity here and they start buying on the second candle in this case. This makes the price to grow and launches it above the limit of the previous period. This is one of the numerous proofs that the real power is in the hands of the buyers and that there is a high possibility that the trend will reverse.

Bearish Engulfing

Has the same concept as bullish engulfing. The thing is that sometimes uptrend can stretch so bad that the opening price can even go higher than the current price in the previous candle. Smart and experienced investors usually decide to sell on these occasions. The length of the candle, in this case, shows that the trend can be reversed from an uptrend to downtrend due to the weight of an opinion.

Piercing Candle is a pattern that represents a strong bearish candle that is in a downtrend. This candle with another, following candle, opens up at a price that is lower than the current one. However, the candle is rallying to have the finishing price, which has the same trading range as the previous day. This pattern can be seen as a signal for the trend reversal and the reason for that is piercing candle as an indicator that sellers are feeling hopeless. When the low prices go even lower it is an opportunity for those who consider themselves to be smart investors to start buying and to push prices strongly up.

Dark Cloud Cover is a pattern that has entirely the same characteristic as the piercing candle pattern. The only difference is that the dark cloud cover is in an uptrend.

Bullish Harami

This pattern has a name that originated from the Japanese word Harami that means "pregnant". As the name suggests, the reason for this is that according to them these candlestick patterns have a resemblance to the pregnant women. If you happen to encounter the bullish harami it means that the market had a lot of active sellers. However, the other candle indicates that the current price became higher. If the second candle finishes up and provides buying enough pressure, you can see it as a signal that there is going to be a change in the price trend. As usual, the following day is a confirmation checker.

Bearish Harami

When a pattern reaches an end of an uptrend there can be a candle that demonstrates exuberance that some might see as naïve. When the other period opens up and the price is lower continuing to go lower as the day goes by, we can say that it indicates second thoughts in buyers. The most probable income of this situation is that the selling will continue regularly and that everything will be resolved once when the price goes into a downtrend.

Candlestick pattern rules

Candlestick patterns named in this chapter certainly aren't the only one that exists. However, these are the main or the most popular ones that you might find useful during your trading career. Like we mentioned once before, nowadays numerous programs and servers can calculate, estimate and identify any pattern that you are interested in. Keep in mind that trading should never be done based on one strategy or just one resource, which is why we wouldn't recommend that you start trading relying only on the information you gather through the candlestick principle for example. Remember, the validity of the pattern depends on the right trend in which the pattern needs to work in. Also, many other indicators have to be taken into consideration.

Chapter 8

Fundamental Analysis in Option Trading

Fundamental analysis is the one that helps you find unique opportunities for trading options. Just like it is not clever to trade relying just on patterns or just on your hunch, it is also not recommended to make decisions based only on fundamental analysis. However, fundamental and technical analyses combined represent the major aspect of the trading market.

Be mindful of the fact that basic knowledge can only point you in the right direction, but there is a lot of work in front of you to be able to become a successful and confident trader. If we take the stock market as an example we can see that even though there are many similar or equivalent principles that can be applied to every of financial markets, including stock one, there are some unique things such as top-down approach for instance, or looking at the bigger picture before going out to find suitable candidates for trade and so on.

Reviewing the Economy

The first step in fundamental analysis is that you need to be able to determine and review the main weaknesses and strengths of the economy. This step will allow you to recognize underlying trends thus have some expectations on the overall performance of the stock markets. Few indicators show the economy's health and many of them are issued by that economy's government. For example, in the United States, the national employment report is issued by the Bureau of Labor Statistics and it is published on the first Friday of each month. Additionally, you can find information about gross domestic products or GDP for short, which is also issued by the government. However, GDP covers many additional things that might be useful. Some of these are investments, exports, personal consumptions, and expenditures.

The GDP is always closely observed by everyone, especially those on financial markets because the impact on GDP directly influences decisions that set interest rates and these decisions are made by the Federal Open Market Committee otherwise known as FOMC or just ''Feds''. FOMS has meetings eight times per year and these meetings are used for decision making about monetary policies and changes in interest rates. The purpose of this is to have overall control over inflation, on the other hand, it is supposed to stimulate the economy too because its main role is to achieve balance or at least something close to that.

Selecting a sector
One that you get a big picture of the economy; you will be able to drill into the different sectors on the market and in independent companies too. The main reason for you to identify your sector before everything else is that it is better if you find a suitable

company in a sector that is decent. It is a better choice than picking a good company that is in a poor performing market environment.

This way you prevent unnecessarily loses on one side and you improve your chance to have a decent performance on the other. The same principle is applicable if you look for assessing companies or some other shorting opportunities. It is inevitable for the companies to be in a cycle and that very much depends on the economic outlook. For example, even during the recession, you can see that some things such as healthcare, food or even some banal things such as staples do well even if the crisis is serious. Customers are usually inclined to avoid luxury goods. Contrarily, if the recession has ended and the economy tries to pick itself up, there is a tendency that other businesses will flourish and make a profit from regular people who make demands. If possible, you should use the opportunity to examine stock cause in this kind of scenario stocks certainly do well but consumers usually end up with great debts. Additionally, financial stocks are good even if there is volatility in interest rates. In this case, rather than promoting stability, the stock promotes competition.

Selection of the company

Once when you passed through all previous tasks, you can finally take the time and look at which company appears to have the best or the worst assets for you. Earnings, prices, and ratios are one of the most important numbers that the company or its analysts look at. However, there are many others. If you try to compare like with like you will see if the numbers you chose were the right ones.

You will also be able to determine what the typical characteristics of the sector are. Keep in mind that companies don't have grocery chains as big as banks for instance. Fundamental analysis is a kind of analysis that investor finds important but when it comes to trading it is not imperative. The main reason is that there are short-termed which move on the market. This is why we explained thoughtfully technical analysis, which is by far more important than the fundamental one.

Chapter 9

Strategies in Option Trading

As you recall, we already had a short overview of the basic strategies in options trading. However, now that we have passed the majority of the most important aspects of the trade it is time that we talk about these strategies in more detail. Now that you have adopted basic mechanisms of options trading you will be able to follow through any of the mentioned strategies. Of course, we can't explain all existent strategies so we will focus on the most important ones. Hopefully, you will be entertained and excited by the many opportunities that come along with the option trade.

Naked Put

Let's start with an interesting premise that you are a stock investor for instance. The first question that you should be asking yourself is what are you supposed to do if you want to buy a stock but the prices are slightly higher than you want to pay. So, the logical thing is that you think that the stock will have a higher value over time but you also don't want to invest too much money in the beginning and handicap yourself that way.

If you think like most stock investors do, you will probably consult your broker to make sure that you'll be notified when the price of the stock falls to the level in which you'd be comfortable to buy, or that you can at least put a limit order on the stock. This time limit means that the broker will buy the stock that you want only if the price of that stock hits the limit that you have set with the broker. Both of these methods are fine and acceptable because you can get the shares that you want for the price that you want. Now, if you think that you are comfortable with using options, for instance, there is another way. If you choose to use options, you can have a position in the shares thus make a lot more money. This means that instead of waiting for the price to drop to the level in which you will be able to pay for it you can just sell an option by the price that is currently on the market.

The effect of this is the following: First of all, you sell rather than buy. Secondly, now you have gained more money by payment or premium from the option you have sold. If the price of the shares drops down to your level it means that you will have to buy those shares. Since this is the thing that you wanted from the beginning eventually it can be a win-win situation.

However, if the price doesn't drop to your level before it becomes worthless it means that you won't get shares, which are once again the same that it would happen if you have waited for the price to go lower or if you have set the limit for obtaining it. But don't forget, you received the money from the premium and it somehow happened that you don't have to do anything for that money.

Things can get even better. For instance, if the option passes its expiration date and becomes worthless and you still want to buy that same stock, you can just sell other put options and make more profit. After the expiration date passes, there is no way that anybody can stop you from selling the option. Although you don't own the shares of the stock you have put yourself into the same position that would occur if you waited for the prices to go down. More importantly, this way you even collected some profit. So, as you can see, the term ''naked'' actually has little connection with the modern understanding, it just represents the fact that at the moment you have bought the shares but you don't have any real ownership over them.

Covered Call

We have mentioned covered call many times in previous chapters. One of the reasons is simply because this strategy is one of the most widely discussed strategies for option trading in the whole world. So, just like ''naked'' meant that you actually don't have any position in the shares you've bought, the term ''covered'' means the opposite. With this strategy, you do have an interest in the shares that you obtain. If you use a covered call it will allow you to sell a call option for the shares that you already own. Differently, from the ''naked'' strategy this one doesn't need to match ideally with the long-term goals that you have. It all depends on your estimation about the behavior of the shares in the future, and of course, one of the decisive factors is the strike price you choose here. A covered call is considered to be a conservative strategy.

As we already explained in the overview, Covered call gives you a few generated percent for each month so when you sell the option you are actually "covered". If by some chance option is exercised by the buyer then you'd have to buy the supply for those shares at the price you previously chose. Still, a covered call is a strategy that has the aim of selling repeated call options and letting them expire while collecting generated and regular income without any obligation for option fulfillment. In a nutshell- this means that your aim should always be on the shares that would never reach the strike price, thus never be exercised.

It is inevitable to state that this kind of call is a matter of judgment. The main reason for that closer the current value is to the strike price the more valuable the option will be. At the same time as soon as the strike price gets closer to the current price possibility of that option being exercised grows immensely. In case this happens, you are obligated to sell the shares. Keep in mind that one option has coverage for a 100 share and double-check if you have enough coverage for all options that you've sold.

The most frequently used formula to make the most out of the covered call strategy is to sell call options that are labeled "at the money" and shortest the expiration date the better. As you already know "at the money" has a value that is higher from call options that are considered to be "out of the money". The fact that you used the shortest possible expiration date gives you the chance to sell covered calls more often. Don't forget that the highest profit that you can get from the shares in the covered call strategy is the strike price. So if the stock doesn't reach the value that you expected but instead goes down, you could feel a bit disappointed.

Reasons like this should make you even more aware that it wouldn't be wise to write covered calls on a stock that might have negative growth. So you should just make covered calls on stocks that you estimate to be neutral or even slightly bullish.

Once that you buy the stocks, even though you can get the premium by writing the covered call you can lose a significant amount of money if the stock falls. Additionally, the amount of profit that you can get is also limited to strike prices as we already mentioned. This implies that you need to look for a fairly stable stock.

Exercising an American Option
American options that were mentioned above are usually the most common style of options applied to shares. They can be exercised at any point until the option reaches its date of expiration. This is very useful because that way you can lock in the profits you make from the trade without any second thoughts about the price of the shares or if they'll change and you could lose your investment. The real question here is how to know when to exercise options? What is some optimal time to do so? The answer can be somewhat surprising.

There are opinions that it is better to exercise your options earlier. Also, many other strategies can be used to take all of the advantages that a profitable position can offer. The easiest way to understand it better is to talk on the concrete example. Let's say that you bought a call option two months ago. At the moment you purchased it the value of the shares was 140 dollars, the strike price was 145 dollars and you have two months before the call option that you bought reaches its expiration limit. At the moment, the value of the shares now is 150 dollars, which means that the option you have to make some profit is in the money.

Be careful, the temptation of exercising your option and keeping the profit can seem like a perfect solution, even more, if you are not certain if the option will continue to rise and your profit with it. Let's say that you are collecting shares. So you bought 100 shares and each share is 145 dollars worth, which means that the total that you spent on shares is 14.500 dollars. The current worth of those same shares is 15.000 dollars, which means that your direct profit is 500 dollars and it is less than the original cost of the option. Now, let's recap one important thing here.

We said that the worth of option is actually the sum of intrinsic value and its time value. In this particular case, the intrinsic value of your shares is 500 dollars. If you add two months that are left before the options expire there has to be some worth in that too. This kind of value can be found online. So, ultimately, you may sell your option for more than 500 dollars and then realize that you now have a greater profit.

If instead of doing that you planned to exercise the option and keep the shares without taking profit immediately there is no need to do so now. It would be better to just invest these 14.500 dollars at a rate of interest that is risk-free. If the option stays to be in the money and valid you can always just take cash for your shares and additional pocket of two months of interest.

Of course, you mustn't forget that there is always a chance that the stock can go down and that its value can be lower than the strike price which means that you can still cash in your shares but for a weaker price and your profit is still based on the price difference and the interests. If your original idea wasn't to keep the shares after the call option was exercised, and you still wanted to sell them and make a profit immediately, then there is another strategy that you should be familiar with. If we suppose that you estimated that the stock won't go well and that its price will be lower than the strike price, then your original intention was to sell the stock as soon as the option is exercised and you bought the stock at a discount that the market was giving.

You can do another thing now. You can lock in your potential gain and sell a stock short and not exercising the option as you planned at the beginning. Look what are the outcomes. Firstly, if the stock's price goes below the strike price you will still make a profit because you have put a short position. Secondly, if the stock price drops up to the strike price level you just simply have locked all gains that were available to you earlier. So, you either earn money from your short position regardless of the fact that the price is lower than the strike price or you can wait for the price of the stock goes up you will still be able to purchase at the strike price even though the option might expire and it means that you won't gain nothing on your short position.

It is true that you wouldn't have additional profits that would have been yours if you purchased the stock before, at an earlier time, and held it for some time but the point is that you make the same amount of profit that you would have if you exercised the option and then sold the stock right away, which in this example we took to be your original intention. There are many strategies that you can use to increase your profit. Those strategies are based on a simple chase of the options early.

There is one time when you might find it necessary to exercise an option early, that one time is when the stockholder offers you a dividend. For any strategy, you have to do some math and calculate what kind of dividend that would be and is it better to just invest money until the option expires? You should establish how much interest you'd get and how early you should exercise the option in that case. If you own a put option, you should consider exercising your option earlier especially if the stock prices fall significantly and you estimate that there isn't enough time to recover. When you face this kind of situation, you should just put the shares send it to the option writer and go collect money that you made.

Spreads

When we talk about strategies known as spreads you should keep in mind that in this scenario options come on their own. Financial markets that are simpler don't have something equivalent to this concept. Spreads are referred to as strategies that include a minimum of two or more trades. Each trade is structured carefully and it has a certain relationship with one another. This way the level of risk is reduced and the possibility for profit exponentially grows. As it was already mentioned in some of the previous chapters, spreads often mean that one contract is going to be sold so another could be bought. Option trading fabricated many strategies. There are even ''synthetic options'' which are strategies that act look and feel like they are a kind of an asset that exists while in reality, it is a construction made out of many different assets. The most important thing to know about spreads is that your imagination can only limit their vitality

Long Stock with Protective Put

This strategy is also commonly used among traders. Another name for this option trading strategy is a "married put". This strategy is based on the purchase of a long stick and obtaining protection for that stock by buying a put option along with it. This strategy is typical for a bull market. This strategy has risks thus profits higher than all of the above. In fact, if your estimation of the stock price going up turns to be accurate, potential profit in your case isn't limited.

On the other hand, if the price doesn't reach anything but instead drops, your safeguard is a put option that will limit your losses. If the current price goes below the strike price you can use the put option that you have to recover the loss on the stock. The value of the put defines the amount of the money that you can recover thus the degree of insurance that you have is conditioned by factors such as the difference between the put option price and the strike price, etc. You expect to make a profit, which means that you have expectations that the value of the stock will increase not the other way around.

Short Stock with Protective Call

Short stock with the protective call is a strategy that has similar characteristics with the one from the above. The key difference is that this spread is designed for a bear market, and as you can suggest, the key thread of the bear market is the assumption that the prices of the stock are going to fall.

If you trade normally you will just buy a short position on the stock you are interested in, and you will profit as the price goes below the strike price. The only different thing that you do while implementing short stock with a protective call strategy is that you buy a call option additionally. This call option on the stock that you wanted acts as a guarantee once again because it lowers your loss risks if by some chance prices start to go up. Variables that you can use to improve your investment are the expiration date of the option and the relationship between the current price and the strike price. When it comes to the expiration date, the same principle applies as always; the closer the option is to its expiration date the less it will be valuable.

Bull Call Spread

A bull call spread is a type of strategy that is more complex than those that we mentioned before. First of all, this strategy has a different profile often referred to as ''collar''. Another name that is often used for this strategy is the vertical spread. In this context, vertical spread uses just the prices that are lined up vertically on the price chart for options trading.

Also, both losses and profits in bull call strategy have their caps. Let's say that we form a spread while buying a call option at a lower strike price and then selling the higher-priced call option with the condition of the same expiration date. A bull call spread is a very popular strategy and it is mostly used for the markets that are considered to be moderately bullish. Since the option bought at the lower strike price is more expensive than an option that is bought at the higher strike price you have a net debt that allows you to open the bull call spread strategy.

Maximized profit is the main distinction between the strike prices being lee or a net debit. Let's say that the difference between the strike prices is 5 dollars and that the position costs two dollars (net), which means that you will lose two dollars if the market goes against you, or that you will earn three dollars if your estimation was accurate. Now, you might wonder why you would have to complicate when it is much easier to use a long call strategy for this kind of situation instead. Well, there is a catch, the trading costs are lower. However, there is also a disadvantage of limited profit potential so the best moment to use bull call strategy is when you don't have great expectations on profit and when you determine that the market is moderately bullish.

Long Straddle

This is one of the strategies that are described as the one that promises profit regardless of the stock price. Long Straddle is indeed a method that has similar performances but keeps in mind that there isn't such a thing as the strategy that makes money nonstop. Also, a change in price is the main requirement for any kind of trade, even for this one.

The thing is, even if there are good chances to earn money using this strategy regardless of the price going up or down, you will actually lose money if the price stays at the same place. A long straddle is a spread that is most effective for the stocks that become increasingly volatile which means that you know that they will move in some direction but you are not certain which direction that will be. Contrary to the long straddle, there is also a short straddle spread that is the exact opposite because you earn money only if the price stays at a similar level (the price almost doesn't change).

You make a long straddle by purchasing a call option and put option that has the same price and identical expiration date. If you are only buying options the level of risk is set in that way that you can't lose more than the amount of the money you paid for those options. If the price increases significantly, your call options become ''in the money''. On the contrary, your put options, in this case, become worthless. A similar principle happens if the price goes down except that you make money using your put options while the call options expire. The main advantage of this strategy is that you theoretically have unlimited profit possibility regardless of the direction of the price. Differently, the main disadvantage is that to make profit prices have to move significantly. In both cases, the maximum loss is suffered only if the strike price and the stock price are the same at the moment of expiration.

Other Strategies

There are many ways that trades can be combined to give different performances and results. Since this guide is for beginners, the strategies mentioned above are probably more than enough for starters. Some of the common names that you will hear in many other advanced strategies are words such as ''butterfly'' or ''strangle'' and so forth. The point of going through some of the complex strategies was to show that option can be unbelievably flexible and that it will take time to study them to their depths. Be mindful of the fact that strategy that guarantees 100 percent win on the options market hasn't been invented yet.

Every strategy is suitable for some sort of situation and sometimes you might have to use more than one strategy to make a profit. You should never rely on just one source of information or just one strategy, you need to be prepared and always have a backup plan because options trading doesn't come without risks. Always be mindful of the cardinal rule of trading that you should never risk more capital than you can afford.

Conclusion

After we discussed many different topics that are directly connected to the option trading and options in general, we would like to sum up impressions into a bullet list, which can be useful whenever you need a quick peek about trading.

First of all, we would point out that the whole guide was written without relying on any kind of fees. As we already mentioned, fees vary and every brokerage house has its own rules about it.

· Trading options have significant risks. If you are absolutely inexperienced with trading we would recommend talking with a financial advisor before making any decision.

· Always keep in mind that every investment has its own risk and reward rating which means that if the risk is high, the reward will be high too.

· Expiration date of American style options and European style options (the most commonly used ones) is always the third Saturday in the month for American and the last Friday before the third Saturday for European options.

· Phrase ''in the money'' describes that the option has a value higher than the strike price for call options and lower than the strike price for put options at the time of their expiration.

- The most common minimal bid for option sharing is one nickel or 5 dollars per contract. However, some more liquid contracts allow minimal bid to be one dollar per contract.

- 100 shares of the certain stock are actually 1 option contract

- If you pay 1 dollar for an option your premium for that option whether you buy or sell it is 1 dollar per share, which means that the option premium is 100 dollars per contract

- All of the examples in this guide assume that every option order ever mentioned was filled successfully.

- Whenever you want to open a new position you will have to sell or buy on the market to ''open''. The same principle applies if you wish to close your position. You sell or buy to ''close''.

- Phrase Open Interest represents the number of option contracts that are opened at the moment. Logically- more opened contracts mean a bigger number and closed contracts mean a smaller number.

- Volume of the options is the number of contracts that are traded in one single day.

Be careful when signing the contracts; make sure you read all of the trading options.

Made in the USA
Middletown, DE
23 November 2019